THE VATICAN AND THE HOLOCAUST

The Catholic Church and the Jews During the Nazi Era

Edited by

Randolph L. Braham

The Rosenthal Institute for Holocaust Studies
Graduate Center/City University of New York
and Social Science Monographs, Boulder

Distributed by
Columbia University Press
2000

EAST EUROPEAN MONOGRAPHS, NO. DL

Printed in the United States of America

Contents

Introduction

This volume is an outgrowth of the series of lectures offered under the auspices of the Rosenthal Institute for Holocaust Studies at the Graduate School and University Center of the City University of New York during the 1998 fall semester. Devoted to the issue of the *Vatican and the Holocaust*, the lectures—with one exception—were envisioned as reactions to *We Remember: A Reflection on the Shoah*, the statement on the Holocaust the Vatican issued on March 16, 1998.

The exception is the seminal study by Professor Hyam Maccoby of the Leo Baeck College in London, providing a historical-theological overview of the Christian origins of anti-Judaism and anti-Semitism. Originally delivered on March 27, 1985 at a conference held at the Graduate Center on the origins of the Holocaust,* Professor Maccoby's piece is included as a useful scholarly overview, making possible a better understanding of the background and implications of the Vatican document. Cogently arguing that anti-Semitism is deeply embedded in the New Testament, Professor Maccoby demonstrates the linkage between Christian anti-Judaism and the Holocaust. He identifies the three major strands in Christian anti-Semitism as follows:

> The first, derived from Gnosticism, providing the dualism by which Jews are regarded as the people of the Devil; the second, derived from Judaism, providing the concept of the Church as the vehicle of God's promises...; the third, and most important of all, is derived from the mystery cults: the concept of the crucified God who saves the world from the consequences of its sins, and who needs the dark figure of the Sacred Executioner [the Jews] to accomplish his salvific death and to take upon himself the evil but necessary role of murderer, thus assuming the role of acolyte of Satan, the evil god.

My study provides a critical historical-political overview of the Vatican document. Following a summary of the many positive developments in Catholic-Jewish relations since the Second Vatican

---

* The study was originally published in *The Origins of the Holocaust: Christian Anti-Semitism*, Randolph L. Braham, ed (New York: Columbia University Press, 1986), pp. 1-14. The volume also contains the responses to Professor Maccoby's thesis by Dr. Alan T. Davies, Reverend Robert A. Everett, Dr. Eugene Fisher, Rabbi A. James Rudin, and Rabbi Marc Tanenbaum.

Council's landmark *Nostra Aetate* declaration in 1965, it presents a succinct analysis of the document, with special attention to the Vatican's interpretation of the role played by Pope Pius XII and the German Catholic Church during the Nazi era. Finally, it summarizes the landmark statements many national Catholic episcopates issued since the mid-1960s, coming to grips with the basically anti-Jewish stance of their followers during the Nazi era, and laying the ground for a possible historic reconciliation between Catholics and Jews.

The articles by Reverend John F. Morley, Professor of Religious Studies at Seton Hall University, Reverend Franklin H. Littell, Professor of Theology at Temple University, and Rabbi A. James Rudin, National Interreligious Affairs Director of the American Jewish Committee—eminent Catholic, Protestant, and Jewish theologians, respectively—present intellectually diverse but equally well-documented scholarly reactions to the Vatican document. I am deeply grateful for their contributions and cooperation in the preparation of this volume.

I would also like to express my thanks to Dr. Frances Degen Horowitz, President of the Graduate School and University Center for her support of Jewish-related studies at the City University of New York. For their generosity in supporting Holocaust-related studies at the Graduate Center, I am indebted to Gábor Várszegi, President of the FOTEX Corporation, Hungary, and mentor of the "J. and O. Winter Fund"; Elizabeth and Jack Rosenthal, the mentors of the Institute that bears their name; Marcel Sand, Chairman of the Institute's Advisory Committee, and its members, especially Gizella and Arie Edrich, Valerie and Frank Furth, Eva and Norman Gati, Irene and Paul Greenwald, Sheba and Jacob Gruber, and Ann and Gaby Newmark. Finally, I would like to express my gratitude to Professor Egon Mayer, Director of the Center for Jewish Studies at the Graduate Center for his consistent support, and to my wife, Elizabeth, for her editorial assistance.

Randolph L. Braham
New York, NY
February 1999

1

The Origins of Anti-Semitism

Hyam Maccoby

Anti-Semitism, if defined as merely an intense dislike of Jews coupled with a tendency to ascribe a wide range of evils to their agency, did not begin with Christianity: one can cite Manetho, Apion and Seneca. Even the more radical anti-Semitism that sees Jews as the earthly agents of a cosmic force for evil did not begin with Christianity; we can see this syndrome in Sethian Gnosticism, which, as recent research makes probable, existed before the advent of Christianity. But Christianity is the channel through which this radical anti-Semitism was transmitted to the medieval and modern world. The idea of the Jews as the people of the Devil, predestined for an evil role in history, can be found in the Gospels (e.g., *Matthew,* 23, and pervasively in *John*), was fully developed in the writings of the Church Fathers, and was further elaborated in the Middle Ages (see Trachtenberg, *The Devil and the Jews*). Modern anti-Semitism has made full use of this ancient and medieval material.

The question is: What is it in Christianity that lends itself to anti-Semitism? Is it something accidental, not involved in the core of Christian teaching—an unfortunate aberration—or is it something more fundamental? Is Christian anti-Semitism the outcome of a misunderstanding of Christian teaching, or is it essential to the teaching itself?

In recent years the long-cherished solution that anti-Semitism is not to be found in the New Testament, but arose in the Church as a misinterpretation of the New Testament, has proved increasingly hard to sustain. Most serious scholars now admit that it is in the New Testament itself, and the question becomes: How deeply embedded in the New Testament? Is it detachable from the main core of the New Testament's message, or not? Various answers have been given.

The answer associated with Rosemary Ruether is that the anti-Semitism of the New Testament arose from the needs of Christian rivalry with Judaism. In order to cope with the continuing existence of Judaism as an independent religion not acknowledging Jesus as the Messiah, it was found necessary to denigrate Judaism and, consequently, the Jews. The myth was created—and embodied in certain New Testament passages—that the Jews had always been an evil people who had consistently rejected the prophets sent to them by God; the final rejection of Jesus was said to be merely the culmination of this pattern. The prophets of the Old Testament were thus not regarded as Jews, nor credited to Judaism; instead they were regarded as proto-Christians, and the archetypal role given to the Jews was that of rejectionists and backsliders.

This analysis offers some hope for the continuance of Christianity as a religion purged of anti-Semitism. For anti-Semitism enters Christianity, according to this view, in a nonfundamental way as the outcome of religious rivalry, rather than as the expression of any essential doctrine. The solution, then, lies in the recognition of Judaism as an independent religion; some writers (e.g., Gaston and Gager), building on Ruether's analysis, have argued that the basis of such a recognition of Judaism as a religion of independent validity also exists in the New Testament, in the writings of Paul. All writers of the Ruether school, however, agree that the myth of an evil Jewry exists in the later books of the New Testament, including the Gospels, and that therefore some excision or demotion of New Testament material is necessary to the continuance of Christianity.

I welcome the analysis of the Ruether school as a great advance, and an emancipation from the standpoint—still held by the great majority even of those Christians concerned about Christian anti-Semitism—that the New Testament itself is free of anti-Semitism. I hold, however, that the Ruether analysis does not go nearly far enough. Anti-Semitism is much more deeply embedded in the New Testament than this acknowledges; for anti-Semitism is not merely an extraneous outcome of religious rivalry but forms an essential ingredient in the Christian myth of redemption. The Jews have a role to play among the *dramatis personae* of this myth, and are not merely a religious group to be superseded or discredited. It is through the role assigned to the Jews in this drama, and its profound imaginative impact, that anti-Semitism has been transmitted, and has survived in secular form in post-Christian communities such as Nazi Germany and Soviet Russia.

If the Jewish rejection of Jesus were the key to Christian anti-Semitism, there would be no difference in quality between Christian and Muslim hostility to the Jews, since the Jews also rejected Muhammad. In fact, however, there is a world of difference. Muslim hostility to Jews is on the same level as Muslim hostility to Christians, and though this has often led to violence and persecution, there has been no *diabolization* of the Jews in traditional Islamic thinking. (It is true that in very recent times, for political motives, diabolization of the Jews has occurred in Islam but, significantly, it involved material drawn from Christian sources such as the blood-libel and the *Protocols of the Elders of Zion*, since Islamic tradition contains no such materials.)

In Christendom, however, the Jews were diabolized, and this arises not from Jewish rejection of Jesus, but from the Jews' mythic role as the murderers, or deicides, of Jesus. Murder alone would not have produced this diabolization: the judicial murder of Socrates by the Athenians, for example, had no such outcome. But the alleged judicial murder of Jesus by the Jews (which is historically incorrect) was combined with the deification of Jesus, so producing the mythic crime of deicide. Even this would not have produced the depth of loathing and metaphysical fear involved in anti-Semitism, were it not that the death of Jesus was mythologized as a *cosmic sacrifice,* so that the Jews figure in the myth as the sacrificers of God. Though they do not intend his death as a sacrifice, but rather act from motives of malice, they bring about a necessary death that functions as salvific for members of the Christian Church.

The Jews thus figure in the central Christian myth of salvation in a role that can be paralleled elsewhere in mythology. A god who brings salvation by his death is often coupled with an evil power or god who brings about the necessary death: thus Osiris is killed by Set, Baal by Mot, Baldur by Loki. The figure of Judas, in the Gospels, has just this quality of fated evil; but Judas is merely the eponymous representative of the Jewish people as a whole, and has been so understood throughout the history of Christian anti-Semitism. Judas betrays Jesus because Satan "enters" him, and Satan is the evil deity who strictly corresponds to Set, Mot or Loki. The Jews are his *earthly acolytes,* and are regarded as Satanic. The role of Satan as engineer of the death of the divine Sacrifice has no analogy in Judaism, and therefore the Christian Satan is a new creation of Christian mythology, with analogies only in pagan sacrificial myths.

Mythology has its roots in anthropology, and we may ask: What was the ritual in which myths of the slaying of a good god by an evil god were grounded? The answer is to be found in rituals of human sacrifice. Where a human sacrifice is performed at times of great stress (especially at the foundation or threatened destruction of a city or a tribe), the guilt for the actual deed of spilling blood was often shifted to the figure of an Executioner, who was cursed and driven into the desert but retained some sanctity as the performer of the deed that saved the tribe. The story of Cain is the remnant of such a ritual. With its abhorrence of human sacrifice, the Hebrew Bible changed the sacrifice of Abel into plain murder; yet with the immunity of Cain, it preserves a feature of the original story. When the Church Fathers identified the Jews with Cain and Jesus with Abel, they sensed the sacrificial overtones of the Cain and Abel story.

The Jews perform the role of Sacred Executioner for Christian society, and this accounts for the strange mixture of loathing and awe that characterizes anti-Semitism. When the Executioner of the divine sacrifice is cursed and driven into the desert, the tribe washes its hands—like Pilate—of the responsibility for the murderous deed that has brought their salvation. Since the tribe depends utterly on the death of the victim for its salvation, it *wants* him to die. But this desire inspires great guilt, which is projected as hatred onto the person deputed to perform the sacrifice. The more the executioner is hated and cursed, the more the tribe feels absolved for the murder which, in reality, they have themselves arranged.

The remedy to anti-Semitism does not lie in cosmetic excisions of "rejectionist" passages in the New Testament, nor in exhortations to recognize Judaism as an independent religion, much as these measures are to be welcomed. It lies in radical criticism of the central Christian myth of salvation, as a means of shifting guilt and responsibility: the main burden of guilt is transferred to Jesus himself, but the secondary guilt involved in the sacrifice itself is shifted to the Jews. Areas to be tackled are: the deification of Jesus; the concept of atonement; the Jews as embodiments of the worst in human nature, or as representatives of Satan. Post-Christian secular versions of anti-Semitism should be analyzed through their relationship to the Christian myth, and treated as "rationalizations," by which the main elements of that myth are given a would-be scientific rationale.

So far in this paper I have given a quick survey of my view of anti-Semitism as a phenomenon rooted in a religious myth. In what follows, I will go into certain aspects of the matter in more detail in order to give a more rounded picture of my thesis and of its possibilities as a program for research and education. It is my view that there are three main elements in Christian anti-Semitism: one derived from Gnosticism, one from Judaism, and one from mystery-religion.

I mentioned earlier that Christianity was not alone in the ancient world in describing the Jews as the agents of a cosmic force for evil, as this had already been done in certain Gnostic sects. Is there, then, a historical connection between Gnostic anti-Semitism and that of Christianity? I believe that there is, and am currently engaged in a research project for the Hebrew University of Jerusalem to establish this connection. Gnostic anti-Semitism may be seen, for example, in the pre-Christian Sethian document *The Apocalypse of Adam*. The characteristic myth of Gnostic anti-Semitism is that the world was created by an evil God, the Demiurge, who in giving the Torah to the Jews made them his chosen people; but that nevertheless, the true High God transmitted the true *gnosis* (tradition of knowledge) through a line of initiates beginning with Seth. Characteristically, Gnostic anti-Semitism selects from the Hebrew Bible non-Jewish personalities, such as Seth, Enoch, or Melchizedek, as the guardians and transmitters of a tradition of knowledge, or gnosis, which rivals and surpasses the Torah, and relegates the Jews to an inferior position as the acolytes of a false God. Because of its Jewish content, drawn from the Hebrew Bible, Gnosticism has sometimes been described as Jewish in origin. A better understanding of the matter, in my view, is that Gnostic anti-Semitism arose among Hellenistic non-Jewish groups who were fascinated by the Hebrew Bible and the claims of the Jews to chosenness, but who reacted by turning the Jewish material on its head and thus produced an anti-Semitic myth. I believe this is a case of cultural rivalry and envy; an ambivalent love-hate relationship to Judaism led to a myth expressing the desire to supplant and usurp the Jewish position as favorites of God, but co-opted Jewish literature to create such a myth. Once fashioned, the myth acts both as a vehicle for aggressive feelings toward the Jews and as a powerful agent of anti-Semitic propaganda, which without the myth's broad imaginative appeal would remain on an abstract level.

The Christian anti-Semitic myth is partly adapted from the Gnostic anti-Semitic myth. The Torah is described not as evil, but as limited. It was not given by an evil God, but by limited supernatural beings, angels, to show that it was intended to have a limited validity. The world was not created by an evil God, but fell under the rule of one, Satan ("the Prince of this world"), and the Jews, by continuing to revere the Torah after its validity ceased, have become the minions of Satan. Thus Christianity presents a moderate form of the dualism of the Gnostic myth, somewhat watered down, but still retaining the anti-Semitic picture of the Jews based on Biblical materials.

On the other hand, another aspect of the Gnostic myth is not watered down in Christianity, but accentuated. This is the supersessionary, or "replacement," element. Gnosticism provided a rival or alternative tradition to that of Judaism; instead of the Jewish succession of prophets, an alternative was posited, a succession of lone voices, bearers of *gnosis* pointing to an other-worldly solution to the ills of this world. Christianity, on the other hand (and this is Rosemary Ruether's main contribution to the study of Christian anti-Semitism), carried out a much larger usurpation. It took over the Jewish prophets themselves, as Christians or proto-Christians. It also took over the whole historical sweep of Judaism—its plan of world history from the creation of Adam to the Last Days—thus giving Christianity a kind of universalism lacking in Gnosticism, which had a historical succession of lone figures but no sense of the historical mission of a community. Islam later carried out a similar usurpation from both Judaism and Christianity: Abraham was represented as a Muslim, and the story of the Akedah was reworked with Ishmael—ancestor of the Arabs—instead of Isaac as the central figure. This element of usurpation is thus a powerful source of anti-Semitism, as Ruether argues; but, in itself, is no greater than the similar process in Islam which produced Muslim anti-Semitism and anti-Christianism. This I would describe as the second element in Christian anti-Semitism—the element derived from Judaism itself, the incorporation of the Jewish historical scheme, necessitating the ousting of the Jews themselves from this schema.

Also, it should also be pointed out that the Gnostic supersessionary method of the *alternative* tradition is not entirely lacking in Christianity, in the use of Biblical non-Jewish personalities, such as Melchizedek and Enoch, to demonstrate the existence of a non-Jewish *gnosis* superior to the Torah.

The third and deepest element in Christianity, with which I am myself concerned in *The Sacred Executioner,* is that derived from the mystery-cults. This element introduces into Christianity a type of anti-Semitism that is more virulent than that of the Gnostic cults. In the Gnostic myth, a succession of redeemer figures is pictured as descending into the world and sometimes suffering persecution at the hands of the Jews; but this is not a central feature, and the main aim of the redeemer is to impart *gnosis,* not to suffer a sacrificial death. Christianity, however, has given a central position to the element of violence. The redeemer figure of Gnosticism has been amalgamated with the redeemer figure of the mystery-cults, in which a dying-and-resurrected god brings immortality to his worshippers by his sacrificial death. The mystery-cults themselves were *not* anti-Semitic, since the figure of the Sacred Executioner in them was that of a rival god, and no human group was identified as this god's acolyte. The anti-Semitism of the Gnostic sects identified the Jews, a recognizable human group, as the enemies of *gnosis,* but it was left to Christianity to deepen the guilt of the Jews by turning the redeemer into a unique sacrificial figure rather than one of a succession of bringers of *gnosis.* The uniqueness of Christianity lies precisely in this amalgamation of Gnosticism with mystery-religion to form an anti-Semitic myth of unprecedented potency. The mystery-cults were local in their reference. Gnosticism, on the other hand, was a universal belief, providing a way of salvation for all mankind, and speaking to the human condition itself. This universality (of a cosmic, not historical, type) gave the Jews an evil universality, as representatives of cosmic evil and enemies of the universal solution to the human problem. This universality was taken into Christian anti-Semitism, with the extra dimension given by the concept of a unique redeemer who saved mankind not through gnosis but by his sacrificial death brought about by the powers of evil through the instrumentality of the Jews.

By what steps, then, was the Christian anti-Semitic myth established? Jesus himself, and his earliest followers in the Jerusalem Church (so-called, for it was not really a church), had no notion of any anti-Semitic myth, for they were practicing Jews themselves and were looking forward to a messianic age, or kingdom of God, in which the Jews would be the honored priest-nation of the world, not cosmic villains. Jesus, in my view, never thought of himself as a divine figure, but as the promised king-messiah who would restore Jewish independence and inaugurate an era of world peace, as prophesied by Isaiah and Zechariah. His enemies, therefore, were not the Jews but the Romans, whose military empire stood in the way of the messianic era of world peace. His death was not regarded by either him or his Jewish followers as a divine sacrifice to atone for the sins of mankind.

It was Paul who created the Christian myth by deifying Jesus for the first time, and by regarding his death as a cosmic sacrifice in which the powers of evil sought to overwhelm the power of good, but, against their will, only succeeded in bringing about a salvific event. We find already in the writings of Paul the concept of the Jews as the unwitting agents of salvation, whose malice in bringing about the death of Jesus is turned to good because this is the very thing needed for the salvation of sinful mankind. The combination of malice and blindness described here is the exact analog of the myth of Baldur, in Norse mythology, in which malice is personified by the wicked god Loki and blindness by the blind god Hother, and both together bring about the salvific death, which alone guarantees a good crop and salvation from death by famine. Thus Paul is the creator of the Christian myth, in that he, by an imaginative stroke, combined the salvation aspect of the mystery-religions with the universality and dualism of the Gnostic cults, thus incidentally also creating cosmic villains, the Jews, while retaining the historical salvation scheme of Judaism. This whole conception arises from Paul's depoliticization of the historical Jesus, by which he was divested of all political attributes as a Jew of his period, and turned into an ahistorical figure, a visitant from outer space with a purely spiritual mission devoid of political content. This was called a "stroke of genius" by Bousset in that it diverted Christianity from conflict with Rome, which was no longer the enemy, being merely a political entity. Instead, on the spiritual plane, the Jews became the enemy; though this anti-political stance was itself an astute political move, since it substituted a defeated, weak political entity, the Jews, as the archetypal enemy in place of a powerful political entity, Rome. The way was thus prepared for an accommodation between Pauline Christianity and Rome, and even for the adoption by Rome of Christianity as its official faith, with its center at Rome itself—an outcome which the loyal Jew, Jesus, with his veneration of Jerusalem as the spiritual center of the world, would have found astonishing and dismaying.

The myth adumbrated by Paul was then brought into full imaginative life in the Gospels, which were all written under the influence of Paul's ideas and for the use of the Pauline Christian Church. A fully rounded narrative of mythological dimensions is now elaborated on the basis of historical materials, which are adapted to provide a melodrama of good and evil. The powerful image of Judas Iscariot is created: a person fated and even designated by his victim, Jesus, to perform the evil deed, possessed by Satan and carrying out his evil role by compulsion, yet suffering the fate of the accursed—a perfect embodiment of the role of the Sacred Executioner, deputed to perform the deed of blood, yet execrated for performing it. While Judas performs the role on the personal level, the Jewish people performs it on the communal level: actuated by blindness and malice in alternation, calling for Jesus' crucifixion in the climactic Barabbas scene and accepting responsibility for the sacrifice by saying: "His blood be on us and on our children!" (*Matthew*, 27:25.) What in Paul's letters was just the outline of a myth has become definite and replete with narrative quality, an instrument for cultural indoctrination and the conveyor of indelible impressions to children who are told the tale. At the same time, the responsibility is carefully removed from the Romans: their cruel, rapacious rule of Judea is softened into a benevolent paternalism, and their chief representative, Pontius Pilate (who was actually a blood-thirsty money-grubber), is represented as well-meaning and mild. All political aspects of Jesus are obliterated (being shunted into the invented person of his *Doppelgänger* Jesus Barabbas), and thus the sole responsibility for his death is laid at the door of the Jewish leaders. To this end, fictitious religious conflict between Jesus and the Pharisees is introduced, and his conflict with the High Priest, which was actually political, is represented as religious. Jesus, by being made into an atoning sacrifice in a cosmic war between good and evil, has been removed from all political realities and from the actual circumstances of his death. The whole story, by being removed to the mythological level, has mythologized the Jews too.

In the subsequent history of the Church, the mythological role of the Jews as deicides and sacrificers of the incarnate God is elaborated and the Jews are further demonized. This process took several centuries to accomplish fully, for ordinary Christians tended at first to treat Jews as ordinary human beings with whom they could have normal social relations. Several councils of the Church forbade such social relations, and great Christian preachers such as St. John Chrysostom denounced all friendliness towards the Jews and built up the picture of the Jews as an accursed nation with whom no Christian should fraternize. Yet the Jews, as they were placed more and more in the role of a pariah class in Christendom (by being forbidden to take part in all normal vocations), fulfilled a societal role, just as they filled a necessary role in Christian mythology. Their role was similar to that played in Hindu society by the Untouchables, except that the latter do the physical dirty work of society, while the Jews, in the Christian economy, do the moral dirty work, which is regarded as necessary, but unfit for Christians. It was necessary to have a class of damned persons available to perform this work. Thus the Jews were pushed into the activity of "usury," forbidden by the Church, but actually essential to the economy. In many areas, the Jews were forced to provide the public executioner of criminals; who better than the Jews, the performers of the necessary murder or execution of Jesus, to perform the official bloodshed of Christian society?

The performance of a necessary function, however hated and despised, was a kind of protection to the Jews. By being always present as the suffering culprits, paying endlessly for their murder of Jesus, they lifted the guilt of that murder from Christians, who by venting their moral indignation on the Jews could feel themselves to be accepted by Christ. Moreover, a saying of Paul gave rise to the belief that the Second Coming of Christ could only occur when the Jews became converted to Christianity; this belief saved the Jews from annihilation on many occasions. At the time of the Second Coming, however, it was believed that the Jews would disappear, either by being absorbed into the Church as converts, or (a more sinister alternative) by being annihilated in the wars of the Antichrist against Christ at the time of his Second Coming. The latter alternative was held by millenarian sects, and had respectable backing in Christian literature, but was on the whole frowned on by the official Church, as it led to populist outbreaks that could turn against the Church itself and its temporal leaders.

At the time of the Second Coming, the Jews would no longer be necessary, because the sacrifice of Jesus would no longer be necessary. Christ Triumphant appears when the problem of human sin (which gave rise to the need for a divine sacrifice in the first place) has been finally conquered. When a suffering Jesus on the cross is no longer needed, a demonic people acting as his accursed executioners is also no longer needed; they can disappear, either by conversion or by annihilation. At times of millenarian excitement, the method of annihilation was indeed tried; this was the aim of the mobs who carried out huge massacres of Jews at the time of the Crusades. Millenarian movements often contained the scenario that the Antichrist would be a Jew who would be hailed by the Jews as their Messiah, and would actually set up a Jewish Empire based on a rebuilt Temple in Jerusalem, but would be defeated by the armies of Christ, when the Jews would be annihilated to the last man. This scenario lies behind the secular, post-Christian millenarian movement of Hitler, in which Hitler himself took the role of Christ Triumphant, and in which many of the slogans of Christian millenarianism—including the "Thousand Year Reich"—were employed.

Post-Christian anti-Semitism can thus be more dangerous to the Jews than Christian anti-Semitism itself, for in post-Christian anti-Semitism, the moral restraints of Christianity have disappeared, and the naked myth of the demonized Jews remains, in an atmosphere of populist millenarianism where the possibility of a pure, *Judenrein* Utopia is envisaged. In the Christian Churches themselves, a new spirit of awareness of Christian responsibility for anti-Semitism already exists, though it has not yet sufficiently reached the lower levels of teaching; nor is the harm done by the simple outlines of the Christian myth sufficiently realized, but on the contrary, it is thought that the beauty of the Christian myth as an edifying story has survived the onslaughts of modern Biblical research. It is only when the phenomenology of the myth itself—quite apart from the question of its historical inaccuracy—is subjected to searching criticism that real progress will be made in combating anti-Semitism, and that this endeavor will be of benefit not only to Christians, but also to post-Christians of every kind, whether of the Left or the Right, or of middle-of-the-road liberal agnosticism, all of whom are more affected than they think by the Christian myth as it relates to the Jews, whom they have not yet succeeded as seeing as normal human beings rather than as actors in a nightmare mythological drama.

To sum up, then, I would argue that there are three strands in Christian anti-Semitism: the first, derived from Gnosticism, provides the dualism by which the Jews are regarded as the people of the Devil; the second, derived from Judaism, provides the concept of the Church as the vehicle of God's promises moving through history from the Creation to the Last Days, and this brings Christianity into collision with the community of Israel from whom these claims are usurped; the third, derived from the mystery-cults and the most important of all, is the concept of the crucified God who saves the world from the consequences of its sins, and who needs the dark figure of the Sacred Executioner to accomplish his salvific death and to take upon himself the evil but necessary role of murderer, thus assuming the role of acolyte of Satan, the evil god. Out of this came the cry, "Who killed Christ?" This is the cry that was heard at the time of Hitler's Holocaust and at every other massacre of Jews in Christendom. This is the reason that Hitler's massacre of the Jews met with silent acquiescence from the vast majority of his subjects. Though public outcry and protests from the Pope brought a quick end to Hitler's program for the extermination of the insane and unfit, no such outcry or protest was forthcoming about the Jews. For it is endemic in Christendom that the Jews, the murderers of God, deserve all possible sufferings.

Bibliography

Wilhelm Bousset, "Antichrist," in: *Encyclopaedia of Religion and Ethics,* John Hastings, ed. (Edinburgh: T. & T. Clark, 1908), Vol. 1, pp. 578-81.

Alan T. Davies, ed., *Antisemitism and the Foundations of Christianity* (New York: Paulist Press, 1979).

John C. Gager, *The Origins of Anti-Semitism* (New York: Oxford University Press, 1983).

John Hick, ed., *The Myth of God Incarnate* (London: SCM, 1978).

Hyam Maccoby, "Jesus and Barabbas," *New Testament Studies,* Cambridge, Vol. xvi, 1968, pp. 55-60.

_____. *Judaism on Trial: Jewish-Christian Disputations in the Middle Ages* (East Brunswick: Associated University Presses, 1982), pp. 19-94.

_____. *Revolution in Judaea* (New York: Taplinger, 1980).

_____. *The Sacred Executioner* (London/New York: Thames & Hudson, 1982), pp. 97-186.

Rosemary Ruether, *Faith and Fratricide* (New York: Seabury Press, 1974).

Herman L. Strack, *Das Blut im Glauben und Aberglauben,* 8th ed. (Leipzig: J. C. Hinrichs, 1911; Schriften des Institutum Judaicum in Berlin, Nr. 14). English version: *The Jew and Human Sacrifice.* Translated by H. Blanchamp. (London: Cope and Fenwick, 1909).

G. Stroumsa, *Another Seed: Studies in Sethian Gnosticism* (Leiden: E.J. Brill, 1984).

Joshua Trachtenberg, *The Devil and the Jews* (New York: Harper & Row, 1966).

.

2

The Vatican:
Remembering and Forgetting
The Catholic Church and the Jews
During the Nazi Era

Randolph L. Braham

The Dramatic Turnaround in Catholic-Jewish Relations

On March 16, 1998, the Vatican issued its long-awaited statement on the Holocaust and Christian-Jewish relations. Titled *We Remember: A Reflection on the Shoah*,[1] the document is generally viewed as the culmination of a series of positive steps the Vatican has taken since the mid-1960s toward improving Christian-Jewish relations in general and combating the scourge of racism and anti-Semitism in particular.

Nostra Aetate

After nearly nineteen centuries of generally venomous anti-Jewish hostility, hatred, and persecution, the Catholic Church began to radically change its position toward the Jews in 1965, when the Second Vatican Council,[2] acting under the leadership of Pope John XXIII, adopted the landmark *Declaration on the Relationship of the Church to Non-Christian Religions*.[3] Better known as *Nostra Aetate* (In Our Age), the document is devoted to fostering "unity and love among men." It summarizes the Church's position on all major organized religions, devoting a lengthier section to its relationship with "the chosen people" (Section 4). Under its provisions, the Church:

- Recognized the common heritage of Christians and Jews—the Church's spiritual and temporal-historical relatedness to Judaism;

- Recommended that in light of this heritage, "biblical and theological studies and brotherly dialogues" be undertaken to foster mutual understanding and respect;

- Admitted that the death of Christ "cannot be blamed upon all the Jews then living, without distinction, nor upon the Jews of today," rejecting the commonly held and widely propagated view that the Jews as a people were eternally guilty for the crime of deicide; and

• Deplored "the hatred, persecutions, and display of anti-Semitism directed against the Jews at any time and from any source."

This historical document retained two negative references to Jews, reflecting the doctrinal constraints under which the bishops operated. Although these references were tempered by the assertion that "the Jews still remain most dear to God," they clearly introduce a discordant note to an otherwise highly positive document. The bishops found it necessary to repeat some doctrinal positions that were the source of many anti-Jewish outbursts in the past. It reasserts that a large number of Jews not only failed to accept but actually opposed the spreading of the gospel, and that the Jewish authorities and their followers had pressed for the death of Christ. While understanding the predicament of the bishops, many Jews and Christians deplored the inclusion of these negative references as well as the failure to recognize the historical responsibility of the Church for the spread of anti-Judaism and anti-Semitism. In light of the Holocaust, they also regretted the absence of an apology or request for forgiveness.

The shortcomings of *Nostra Aetate* in treating the wrongs of the past are counterbalanced by the very positive orientation it portends for the future. The Declaration has forever changed Christian-Jewish relations for the better. The mutual suspicions that characterized these relations before 1965 have been replaced by dialogue and understanding in most parts of the Christian world. There have been more positive encounters between Catholics and Jews in the few decades after 1965 than ever before during the long history of the Catholic Church. *Nostra Aetate* was followed by other important Vatican and national Catholic Church documents which reinterpreted parts of the New Testament and eliminated many anti-Jewish references in Catholic textbooks, teachings, and liturgy.

Impact of Pope John Paul II

Most of the changes leading to the further improvement of Christian-Jewish relations were initiated by Pope John Paul II, who is generally regarded as highly conservative on doctrinal matters. More than any other Pope in history, it was this Polish-born Pontiff who openly talked about—and asked forgiveness for—the sins, crimes, and errors that were committed in the name of the Church. Karol Wojtyla, the future Pope, was raised in southern Poland, where he witnessed not only the brutal oppression of his country by the Nazis but also the systematic destruction of the Jews, including many of his friends and acquaintances. It is generally assumed that the Pope's commitment to the eradication of racism and anti-Semitism stemmed from his wartime experiences. Since his elevation to the temporal and ecclesiastical leadership of the Roman Catholic Church in 1978, the Pope has initiated an impressive number of symbolic and substantive measures not only to combat the scourge of racism and anti-Semitism, but also to improve Catholic-Jewish relations. Not all the utterances and actions of Pope Paul II were applauded by the Jewish community;[4] nevertheless, a number of them stand out, among many others, as landmarks toward Catholic-Jewish reconciliation. For example, the Pope:

- Referred to the Holocaust as "the Golgotha of our century" during a visit to Auschwitz in 1979;

- Became the first Pope in modern times to enter a Jewish house of worship when he visited the Rome synagogue in 1986;

- Assured the leaders of the Jewish community in Strasbourg in 1988 of his "strongest condemnation of anti-Semitism and racism, which are opposed to the principles of Christianity";

- Was instrumental in the preparation of "The Church and Racism," a document issued in February 1989 by the Pontifical Commission for Peace and Justice. The document identified anti-Semitism as "the most tragic form that racist ideology has assumed in our century" and warned—for the first time ever—that anti-Zionism "serves at times as a screen for anti-Semitism";

- Established diplomatic relations between the Vatican and the State of Israel in 1994;

- Hosted a concert at the Vatican in commemoration of the victims of the Holocaust in 1994;

- Issued once again, on the fiftieth anniversary of the liberation of Auschwitz on January 29, 1995, a strong condemnation of anti-Semitism, calling the Holocaust "a darkening of reason, of conscience, of the heart";

- Admitting on October 31, 1997 that certain Christian teachings, based on "erroneous and unjust" interpretations of the New Testament, had helped contribute to the Holocaust and the persecution of Jews in Europe over the centuries, he also asserted that "anti-Semitism has no justification and is absolutely reprehensible";[5] and

- Told a group of Austrian dignitaries and officials during a visit to Vienna on June 30, 1998 that European Christians had a moral obligation to fully reconcile with the Jews, again emphasizing the Jewish origins of Jesus Christ.[6]

The "We Remember" Document

Positive Features

The Vatican document clearly reflects the ideas and doctrinal positions of Pope John Paul II. It is bound to emerge not only as an effective educational tool for the advancement of tolerance and pluralism but also as a formidable weapon in the struggle against the falsifiers of history in general and the Holocaust in particular. It incorporates, among other things, a moving call to penitence, a denunciation of racism and anti-Semitism, and an expression of regret over the Holocaust. The document has justly been praised by many Jews and Christians alike for:

- The forthrightness with which the Pope, in his cover letter, identified the Shoah as "an indelible stain on the history of the century" and "an unspeakable iniquity";

- Expressing the need to remember the Shoah and the inhumanity with which the Jews were persecuted and massacred;

- Acknowledging the impact of the "erroneous and unjust interpretations of the New Testament regarding the Jewish people";

- Admitting the anti-Jewish measures that stemmed from the "sentiments of anti-Judaism in some Christian quarters" and "the gap which existed between the Church and the Jewish people";

- Deeply regretting the silence of Christians who had witnessed the Holocaust, identifying it as a heavy burden of conscience that called for penitence;

- Unequivocally reaffirming the *Nostra Aetate* declaration by stating that the Church "deplored the hatred, persecutions and display of anti-Semitism directed against the Jews at any time and from any source;" and

- Committing the Church to preventing "the spoiled seeds of anti-Judaism and anti-Semitism" from ever again "taking root in any human heart."

Criticisms

Although *We Remember* is clearly one of the most important landmarks in Catholic-Jewish relations, it failed to receive general and unequivocal approval. Many of its critics assert that instead of offering an apology, the document is in fact an apologia of the Catholic Church. By far the most critical comments relate to the perceived attempt by the leaders of the Vatican to: absolve the Church of any responsibility for the Holocaust; differentiate between Christian anti-Judaism and Nazi anti-Semitism; reflect the wartime attitude of the Christians in a positive light; emphasize the alleged anti-Nazi position of the German Catholic Church leaders; and highlight Pope Pius XII's positive role during the Nazi era. What follows is a succinct overview of the former three and a more extensive analysis of the latter two criticisms.

Reflecting the views of Pope John Paul II, the Vatican document, like *Nostra Aetate*, absolves the Church of any responsibility for the role it played in the persecution of the Jews during its long history.[7] It places blame exclusively on "the errors and failures of [its] sons and daughters" for the persecution endured by the Jews. The document justifies the absolution of the Church by differentiating it from its members. Quoting the Pope, it states:

> In the Christian world—I do not say on the part of the Church as such—enormous and unjust interpretations of the New Testament regarding the Jewish people and their alleged culpability have circulated for too long, engendering feelings of hostility toward this people.[8]

The historical record suggests that while the level of persecution varied from country to country, it was the anti-Judaism and anti-Semitism propagated as official Church dogma that induced many Christians throughout Europe to accept, condone, and frequently applaud the ever harsher measures against the Jews, including those that dealt with the Final Solution during the Nazi era. The Jews were not only "looked upon with a certain suspicion and mistrust" for having clung to "their religious traditions and communal customs," as the Vatican document asserts, but were in fact subjected to a relentless institutionalized policy of humiliation, discrimination, hatred, and persecution—an ecclesiastical policy that was often supported and abetted by temporal local, regional, and national governments in almost all countries of Christian Europe.

In defending the infallibility of the Church as a sacrosanct institution, the document also offers a clear distinction between Christian anti-Judaism and Nazi anti-Semitism. It aims to defend the institutional integrity of the Church by highlighting the fundamental differences between Christian anti-Judaism and the racism of the Nazis. While asserting that "the Shoah was the work of a thoroughly modern neopagan regime," the document—in another attempt to absolve the Church—self-righteously claims that the Nazis' "anti-Semitism had its roots outside of Christianity." It clearly aims to advance the belief that the anti-Semitism of the Holocaust era had no Christian roots. Ample historical evidence allows us to infer that without the demonization of the Jews during the long history of the Church, the Holocaust might not have happened. By delegitimizing the Jews and Judaism, Christian anti-Judaism in fact laid the groundwork for the neopagan anti-Semitism of the Nazis. It is this long history of Christian anti-Judaism and anti-Semitism that determined the basically inimical attitude of most European Christians during the Holocaust.

While admitting that the propagation of anti-Judaism during the centuries had a harsh impact on the Jews living in the Christian world—a world in which they were often subjected to persecution, forced conversion, ghettoization, and expulsion—the Vatican document places exclusive responsibility for the Holocaust on Nazi racial anti-Semitism.[9] In differentiating between Christian anti-Judaism and Nazi anti-Semitism, the document overlooks the fact that the Nazi onslaught against the Jews took place in a climate of opinion that was conditioned by centuries of Christian hostility to the Jews.[10] Many clergymen, both before and during the Nazi era, virtually intoxicated the masses with the venom of anti-Judaism and anti-Semitism by portraying the Jews as a people who had betrayed God and had become forever cursed for the crucifixion of Jesus. As Jules Isaac, the well-known French-Jewish scholar, aptly remarked: "Without centuries of Christian catechism, preaching and vituperation, the Hitlerian teachings, propaganda and vituperation would not have been possible."[11] The historical record demonstrates that the rapturous reception of Nazi racial ideology in Germany and elsewhere was to a large extent due to the many centuries of Christian anti-Judaism and anti-Semitism. The linkage between classical Christian anti-Judaism and Nazi anti-Semitism was aptly summarized by Professor John T. Pawlikowski, the noted Catholic theologian as follows:

> *We Remember* leaves the strong impression that there was *no* inherent connection between Nazi ideology and classical Christian anti-Judaism and anti-Semitism. This is basically inaccurate. Among Europe's Christian population, Christian anti-Judaism and anti-Semitism had

everything to do with widespread acquiescence and even collaboration with the Nazi policy devoted to the destruction of the Jews. I like to speak of classical Christian anti-Judaism and anti-Semitism as providing an indispensable "seedbed" for Nazism.[12]

The Vatican document is understandably charitable in its characterization of Christian behavior during the Holocaust when claiming that while many Christians gave "every possible assistance...to the persecuted Jews...others did not." Actually, the historical record demonstrates that while a pitifully few dared to take risks in order to save their Jewish friends or neighbors, for a variety of reasons the overwhelming majority of Christians remained basically passive, and a relatively large number of them actively collaborated with the Nazis in the war against the Jews.[13] Many among the collaborators seemed intoxicated with anti-Judaism and anti-Semitism; many others were driven by rapacious instincts or racist political-ideological considerations.

But serious as these observations about the inadequacy of the document may be, by far the most critical observations have been advanced in connection with its references to the questionable role played by the Catholic Church leaders in Germany, and its failure to forthrightly deal with the policies of the Vatican during the Nazi era, in particular the silence of Pope Pius XII during the Holocaust.

The Catholic Church Leaders of Germany

The Vatican document is extremely evasive and selective in its treatment of the role of the German Catholic Church leaders. It focuses primarily on the doctrinal positions taken by some leaders *before* Hitler's acquisition and solidification of power, denouncing the Nazis' idolatry of race and of the state. It mentions by name only Archbishop Adolf Cardinal Bertram of Breslau, president of the German Bishops' Conference; Michael Cardinal Faulhaber, the titular leader of the Bavarian hierarchy; and Canon Bernhard Lichtenberg, the Provost of St. Hedwig's Cathedral in Berlin. While the document correctly notes that Father Lichtenberg paid with his life in Dachau for having publicly prayed for the Jews, it doesn't mention that reportedly he was the only priest in the Third Reich to have raised his voice in protest against the barbarism of *Kristallnacht*.[14] It understandably also fails to note that in contrast to his position during the Weimar era, Cardinal Bertram later advocated a policy of appeasement of the Nazi regime and maintained cordial relations with the Führer. Upon hearing of the Führer's death early in May 1945, he ordered solemn requiem masses in all his parishes.[15]

While the German Catholic Church leaders largely opposed the National Socialists during the Weimar era on both political and ecclesiastical grounds, they gradually accommodated themselves to the Nazi regime after Hitler's acquisition of power in January 1933. The Vatican document overlooks the enthusiasm with which most of these Church leaders supported the domestic and foreign policies of the Führer during almost the entire National Socialist era.

The Weimar Era

The Catholic Church leaders had been uneasy about the political successes of the National Socialists during the last few years of the Weimar Republic, fearing their possible impact on the interests of the church. Many of them belonged to the German Catholic Peace Union (*Friedensbund deutscher Katholiken*)[16] and provided effective leadership in the enforcement of Church rules, including the prohibition of membership in the Nazi party. They also closely adhered to traditional moral teachings relating to the possible participation of Catholics in hostilities initiated by states, differentiating between "just" and "unjust" wars.

However, many of the same Church leaders were also concerned with the perceived parliamentary weaknesses and liberal shortcomings of the first genuinely democratic republic in the history of Germany. With various degrees of enthusiasm, they sympathized with, if not actually supported, the Nazis' position on the perceived evils of the Weimar Republic. Their views on communism, socialism, liberalism, and freemasonry, all movements having quite a few members or followers who were Jews or of Jewish descent, largely dovetailed with those advocated by the Nazis. Consequently, while these Church leaders were genuinely concerned with some aspects of the National Socialist program, especially those pertaining to State-Church relations,[17] they did virtually nothing to stem the growing tide of anti-Semitism. Some of them even expressed their concurrence with the Nazis' "endeavor to maintain the purity of the German blood and German race" and with their resolve to fight the Jews' "hegemony in finance, the destructive influence of the Jews in religion, morality, literature and art, and political and social life."[18]

The Nazi Era

Shortly after his inauguration as Chancellor of Germany on January 30, 1933, Hitler proceeded with the establishment of the totalitarian regime that would enable him to implement the National Socialist program. The torching of the *Reichstag* on February 27, an act attributed to the Communists, served its purpose. At Hitler's urging, President Hindenburg issued far-reaching emergency decrees virtually abolishing the basic rights and liberties guaranteed under the Weimar constitution. These were promptly exploited for the arrest of many Communists and other opponents of the Nazis. As a result of the elections, held on March 5 amid an atmosphere of intimidation and terror, the Nazis and their political partners, the Nationalists, obtained an absolute majority of 52 percent of the votes. To acquire the two-thirds majority required for constitutional amendments, Hitler felt compelled, temporarily at least, to appease the Catholics. To acquire the support of the Catholic Center party, Hitler made a series of promises and concessions to German Catholicism. On March 23, he issued a policy statement reassuring the Christian churches of his resolve to work for peaceful relations between Church and State. The Catholics were further enticed by Hitler's comments about signing a Concordat with the Vatican—a major objective of the German Catholic Church and of the Vatican. On March 24, Hitler acquired the support of the Catholic Center party for passage of the Enabling Act, under which the power of legislation was transferred from the legislative to the executive branch of the government for a period of four years. The Act enabled Hitler to enact ordinary legislation by decree—a power that was further extended in January 1934, when he was specifically granted the authority to decree constitutional changes.

Driven by its concern for the protection of the prerogatives of the Church, the German Catholic episcopate followed the initiative of the Center party by issuing a declaration on March 28, 1933. In contrast to its earlier position, the episcopate assured the Catholic members of the National Socialist party and movement that they would be admitted to the sacraments "without being harassed on account of their membership."[19] On May 30-June 1, the Fulda Bishops' Conference, the first plenary conference of all German Catholic bishops since 1848, issued a joint pastoral letter under which the episcopate withdrew its earlier prohibitions against membership in the Nazi party and admonished the faithful to be loyal and obedient to the new regime.[20] Accepting Hitler's assurances at face value, they looked upon the National Socialist regime as just another anti-communist authoritarian system, failing to recognize Hitler's totalitarian objectives.

The German Catholics were enthusiastic about the Concordat that the Third Reich and the Vatican signed, after considerable wrangling, on July 20, 1933. This treaty was still another step toward legitimizing the Hitler regime, and, coming after the Center party's support for the Enabling Act and the Fulda Bishop's Conference, virtually sealed the subordination of German Catholics to the Nazi regime.[21]

Encouraged by Hitler's initial domestic and foreign policy successes, the German Catholic leadership adopted an increasingly nationalist posture. With a few exceptions, the bishops and their subordinates gradually became oblivious to the violations of civil rights and liberties and virtually ignored the Nazis' drive against the Jews. Although not always publicly, they would generally approve, if they did not actually applaud, the arrest and imprisonment of communists, socialists, and other leftist opponents of the regime whom they deemed to represent a threat to the Church as well. Again with a few exceptions, their reaction to foreign reports about the terror that was raging with increasing intensity in the Reich was generally not very different from that voiced by the Nazis themselves. Archbishop Conrad Gröber of Freiburg (Breisgau), for example, rejected the external accusations as "slanderous." A leading Catholic Church figure who "did not take at all unkindly to the National Socialist surge to power," became a supporting member (*Förderndes Mitglied*) of the SS. Anti-Nazi Germans reportedly referred to him sarcastically as the "brown[-shirt] bishop."[22] The reference was quite apt: the Bishop's views on the Jews did not fundamentally differ from those advanced by the Nazis. Identifying Marx as a Jew, he characterized Bolshevism as "an Asiatic state despotism ... in the service of a group of terrorists led by Jews." The Führer, in his view, had "correctly described the struggle against this evil force as a defense of European civilization." The German national tradition, Gröber emphasized, was being threatened by Marxism—a movement "led mostly by Jewish agitators and revolutionaries."[23]

The identification of Jews with Bolshevism was but one of many anti-Semitic themes that were exploited by German Catholic clergymen serving the interests of the Nazi regime. Feeding the flames of anti-Semitism, many of them demonized the Jews in their sermons and writings published in journals edited by priests or in books bearing the *Imprimatur*. Throughout the Nazi era, they identified the Jews as "harmful to the German people," and referred to them as Christ killers who, "in their boundless hatred of Christianity were still in the forefront of those seeking to destroy the Church." A veteran National Socialist priest hailed Hitler as "the tool of God called upon to overcome Judaism...."[24]

Hitler himself noted the linkage between these views and those expressed by the Nazis. On April 26, 1933, during one of his few face-to-face meetings with Catholic bishops, Hitler touched upon the Jewish question, emphasizing the fundamental agreement between National Socialism and Catholicism. The Führer claimed that he was merely doing—and would continue to do—what the Church had done for

1,500 years. The Church, he pointed out, had always regarded the Jews as parasites, banished to live in ghettos.[25]

The cooperation between the German Catholic Church and the Nazi regime was not always smooth and trouble-free. After his solidification of power, Hitler proceeded with the implementation of his program, which sometimes clashed with the interests of the Church. Hitler's subtle efforts to "purify" Christianity by removing its Jewish component, to secularize the parochial schools, and to absorb all Church-affiliated children into the Hitler *Jugend*, to cite just a few, were clearly in conflict with his earlier assurances to the Christian churches and in obvious violation of the provisions of the Concordat with the Vatican. It was these issues rather than the drive against the Jews and other opponents of the Nazi regime that aroused the ire of the German Church leaders.

It was basically for the same reasons—the fundamental ecclesiastical interests of the Catholic Church—that Pope Pius XI felt compelled to issue his famous encyclical letter, *Mit brennender Sorge* (With Burning Anxiety). After considerable wrangling among the German bishops, the letter was read from the pulpits in all Catholic churches in Germany on Palm Sunday, March 21, 1937. A number of the bishops, including Bertram, clearly feared that the condemnation of racism by Pope Pius XI, a condemnation emphasized by the Vatican statement on the Holocaust, would elicit a negative reaction on the part of the National Socialist regime.[26] These bishops, who continued to support the regime they had helped solidify, were presumably taken aback by the Pope's assertion that "true belief in God was irreconcilable with the deification of earthly values such as race, people or the state."[27] They apparently failed to realize that the encyclical was an attack not so much on Nazi racism as on the neopaganism favored by the German authorities. The encyclical included neither a condemnation of political and social totalitarianism nor a denunciation of anti-Semitism. In fact, it referred to the Jews as the people "destined to crucify Him," repeating the centuries old libel that was the major source of Christian anti-Semitism.[28] The negative Catholic reaction to racism and the anti-Semitic racial laws adopted in Nazi-dominated Europe was not due to any pro-Jewish sentiments but primarily, if not exclusively, to the desire to protect the vital interests of the Church. The racial laws, including those that prohibited interracial marriage and conversion of Jews to Catholicism, were criticized and occasionally vehemently opposed because "they struck at the exclusive sacramental structure of the Church."[29]

That the German Catholic leaders were not particularly upset about the Nazis' anti-Jewish policies is reflected in their contrasting reaction to Hitler's euthanasia program. While they fought vigorously and successfully against this program, they failed to raise their voices against the Nazis' increasingly draconian measures against the Jews. Like the leaders of the other Christian denominations, they in fact boosted the regime's prestige by applauding the Führer's domestic and international policies. Like the nation as a whole, they were swept away by the wave of nationalism and patriotism that had engulfed the Third Reich.[30] Bending their traditional moral teachings on "just" and "unjust" wars, the Catholic Church leaders identified Hitler's aggressions as *just*, and "impressed upon all the faithful that it was their inescapable moral obligation to perform whatever services the Reich required of them."[31] This obligation to obey, a noted scholar of German Catholicism concluded,

> ... was given such repeated and fervent emphasis that, to all intents and purposes, the Church did become an agency of social control operating in behalf of the Nazi state insofar as insuring wholehearted Catholic support of the war was concerned. [...] In World War II, the leading spokesmen of the Catholic Church in Germany did become channels of Nazi control over their followers, whether by their general exhortations to loyal obedience to legitimate authority or by their even more direct efforts to rally these followers to the defense of *Volk*, *Vaterland*, and *Heimat* as a Christian duty.[32]

In the wake of such exhortations by the ecclesiastical leadership, the followers of the German Catholic Church tended consistently to agree with the Nazis' domestic policies and military engagements, especially during the pre-Stalingrad phase of the war. Deeming them "just," the Church leaders were loud in their support of Hitler's aggressive wars, and were silent over the persecution of the Jews. Driven by racist ideological considerations and rapacious instincts, a large number of their followers actually applauded the Nazis' war against the Jews. Like the German people as a whole, they generally failed to take a public stand either against the injustices of the Nuremberg Laws of 1935 or the barbarism of *Kristallnacht* (November 9, 1938).

By the time Hitler announced his warning against the Jews early in 1939,[33] the German masses had already been virtually immunized against the horrors of the anti-Jewish drive. Agreeing with the nationalist arguments advanced by the leaders of the Third Reich, they generally supported Hitler's aggression against Poland (September 1, 1939) and the simultaneous launching of the drive against the Jews with almost equal enthusiasm. During this first euphoric phase of the war, the frenzy of patriotism that engulfed the Reich made them virtually oblivious to the Nazis' extension of the Final Solution against the

Jews of Germany as well. The machinery of destruction, refined during the first two years of the war, would be shifted into high gear on September 1, 1941, when the Jews of the Reich were compelled to wear the Star of David. The leaders of the Christian churches were concerned almost exclusively with the pastoral care of non-Aryans and the impact that star-wearing converts and Christians (identified as Jews under the Nazi racial laws) might have on Aryan congregants during services. They manifested the same basically negative attitude during the mass deportation of the German Jews which began on October 15, 1941.[34] The barbarism of the deportations notwithstanding, the Church leaders were concerned almost exclusively with the fate of the converts and the non-Aryan spouses of Christians. They maintained the same negative attitude even after they became fully acquainted with the fate of the deported German Jews (most were shot by mobile killing detachments near Riga and Minsk), and with the large-scale massacres the SS and their accomplices perpetrated in the occupied territories, especially in the East.[35]

There were some lower-rank Church figures whose conscience was aroused by the plight of the Jews. Among these were Canon Bernhard Lichtenberg,[36] Margarete Sommer,[37] and the Jesuit Alfred Delp, a member of the German resistance.[38] A few among the Church leaders dared to reveal their anxiety over the anti-Jewish drive only in private communication among themselves. A few found the courage to issue public pronouncements that criticized the treatment of "foreign races" without mentioning Jews by name. As Guenter Lewy, the noted authority on the German Catholic Church, concluded:

> Unlike the case of the extermination of Germans in the euthanasia program, where the episcopate did not mince words and succeeded in putting a stop to the killings, the bishops here played it safe. The effect of their public protests on the Final Solution consequently was nil. These very general statements neither changed the policies of the government nor inspired any change in the behavior of German Catholics. [...] The machinery of extermination continued to function smoothly, with everyone conscientiously doing his assigned job. The episcopate had repeatedly issued orders to exclude from the sacraments Catholics who engaged in dueling or who agreed to have their bodies cremated. The word that would have forbidden the faithful, on pain of excommunication, to go on participating in the massacre of the Jews was never spoken. And so Catholics went on participating conscientiously, along with other Germans.[39]

Even at the end of the war, when all the gruesome details of the Nazis' war against the Jews were already fully known,[40] Adolf Cardinal Bertram, the last Prince Bishop of Breslau and head of the German Bishops' Conference, not only opposed all public protest against the deportations and massacre of the Jews, but continued to see and respect Hitler as the Catholic state head of the Reich. Upon learning of the death of the chief architect of the Final Solution program, on May 2, 1945, Cardinal Bertram instructed all the parish priests of his archdiocese "to hold a solemn requiem in memory of the Führer and all those members of the *Wehrmacht* who have fallen in the struggle for our German Fatherland, along with the sincerest prayers for *Volk* and Fatherland and for the future of the Catholic church in Germany."[41]

The Vatican During the Nazi Era

We Remember provides a few examples of the Holy See's positive stands during the Nazi era, highlighting Pope Pius XI's encyclical of 1937 and his September 6, 1938 statement to a group of Belgian pilgrims. The Pope is quoted as having said: "Anti-Semitism is unacceptable. Spiritually, we are all Semites." The document is silent on why another encyclical the Pope commissioned in June 1938 was never issued. Titled *Humani Generis Unitas* (The Unity of the Human Race), the encyclical incorporated a condemnation of racism and anti-Semitism.[42] Although the planned encyclical retained the Church's traditional litany on anti-Judaism and merely repeated the standard Catholic position on racism and anti-Semitism without condemning the anti-Jewish measures Germany and Italy had already adopted by that time, its issuance might have had a sobering effect on the faithful and perhaps even on the Axis governments. Recognizing that there was a historically long-standing Jewish problem requiring a solution, the document merely repeated the Church's traditional position, stipulating that a true solution required adherence to "the strict requirements of justice and charity." The historical record reveals that the Vatican, like most Christian Church leaders in German-dominated Europe, believed that the avalanche of anti-Jewish measures adopted during the Nazi era had satisfied this requirement.[43]

The policies of Pope Pius XI were continued by his former Secretary of State, Eugenio Cardinal Pacelli, who was elected Pope on March 2, 1939. Pope Pius XII, recognized as a gifted, highly knowledgeable, and industrious individual, was generally regarded as a Germanophile. During his nine years of service as Nuncio in Germany (1920-29), he had acquired a good command of German and developed a special predilection for the German people. The Vatican document on the Holocaust cites Pope Pius XII twice as "proof" of his anti-Nazi position. It emphasizes the Pope's encyclical (*Summi Pontificatus*) of October 20, 1939, in which he "warned against theories which denied the unity of the human race and against the deification of the state," and the expressions of thanks Jewish leaders extended to him after the war for what he did[44] "personally or through his representatives to save hundreds of thousands of Jewish lives."[45]

The historical record shows that the Vatican's position on the National Socialists, both before and after their acquisition of power, and on the persecution of the Jews largely paralleled that of the German Catholic hierarchy. During the Weimar era, Pope Pius XI, like his Secretary of State, echoed the position of the German bishops, condemning anti-Semitism and the Nazi myths of race and blood while adhering to the Church's long-standing doctrine on Judaism. Even after the victory of the Nazis and the consequent adoption of increasingly severe anti-Jewish measures, the Vatican restricted its interventions to the defense of the interests of the Church, which extended to the protection of non-Aryan Catholics. All the initiatives of the Vatican, including the Pope's well-known encyclical of 1937, were taken almost exclusively in response to Hitler's attempt to subordinate the church to the state in violation of earlier commitments and legal obligations, including those provided under the Concordat. The persecution of the Jews was never the subject of an encyclical. The Pope and the top officials of the Vatican were well acquainted with the Nazis' anti-Semitic aims both before and after Hitler's inauguration as Chancellor. These were brought to their attention not only by the nuncios representing the Vatican in many countries, but also by many private individuals. One of these was Edith Stein, the Jewish convert to Catholicism and well-known philosopher,[46] who entreated the Pope to issue an encyclical on the Jewish question. Her plea, like many similar suggestions by Jews and non-Jews in both Nazi Europe and the free world, was left unheeded.

Awareness of the Anti-Jewish Drive

The evidence that the Pope, his Secretary of State Luigi Cardinal Maglione, and the other top officials of the Vatican were fully and accurately informed about the details of the Final Solution program in all Nazi-dominated Europe is both abundant and compelling. Their sources of information were many and reliable. They were kept abreast, among other things, by the nuncios, Catholic and other Christian church officials in many parts of the world, representatives of various major Jewish organizations, and spokesmen for the Allied and neutral countries.[47]

Evidence concerning awareness by the Catholic Church's leadership of the Final Solution was published by the Vatican itself in the 1970s. In its series of volumes on the papacy's role during World War II, the Vatican published a number of documents which, though obviously selective, reveal that Pope Pius XII had received periodic reports through diplomatic and private channels concerning the mass killing of Jews in the USSR, Poland, and the later deportations to death camps from various parts of Nazi-dominated Europe. From the beginning of 1942, the Pope received more detailed reports about the anti-Jewish drive, including the fact that many of the deportees were destined for death. One of the first church dignitaries to alert the Pope about "the terrible fate" of the Jews was the Archbishop of Vienna, Theodor Cardinal Innitzer.

But by far the most reliable reports came in from the nuncios, the representatives of the Vatican.[48] One of the most accurate sources was Monsignor Giuseppe Burzio, the papal envoy in Bratislava, who kept the Vatican informed about the mass deportations from Slovakia from their beginning in March 1942. The Papal Nuncio in Berlin, Archbishop Cesare Orsenigo, reported to Monsignor Giovanni Battista Montini, then Acting Secretary of State to Pope Pius and the future Pope Paul VI, that "the most macabre suppositions about the fate of the non-Aryans are admissible."[49]

One of the main sources of information about the Nazis' designs against the Jews was Archbishop Angelo Giuseppe Roncalli, the Apostolic Delegate in Istanbul (later to become Pope John XXIII). In his report of July 8, 1943, addressed to Monsignor Montini, Archbishop Roncalli stated that millions of Jews had been sent to Poland and annihilated there. He did not elaborate on the annihilation, presumably because the extermination camp system was by then sufficiently well known. Archbishop Roncalli also revealed his knowledge about the exterminations to Franz von Papen, the German Ambassador in Ankara, who replied by citing the Soviet massacre of Poles in the Katyn forest, near Smolensk.[50] One of Archbishop Roncalli's sources of information was the Executive Committee of the Jewish Agency of Palestine, with which he had been in close contact since 1943. The leader of the Agency's delegation in Istanbul, Chaim Barlas, kept the Apostolic Delegate informed about the anti-Jewish measures in Europe.[51]

First-hand information about the Final Solution was forwarded to the Vatican in the summer of 1942. In August, *SS-Obersturmführer* Kurt Gerstein informed Dr. Winter, the legal adviser of Konrad Cardinal Preysing, the Bishop of Berlin, about the gassings he had witnessed at Belzec, near Lublin, and urged that this information be relayed to the Vatican.[52] A few months earlier, the representatives of the domestic and international Jewish organizations in Switzerland gave an interview to Archbishop Filippo Bernardini, the Nuncio in Bern, informing him both orally and in writing about the plight of Jews in

East Central Europe. A Jewish Agency memorandum, outlining the mass deportations from Western Europe and the executions of Jews in Poland, was forwarded to Secretary of State Maglione in September 1942 via Harold H. Tittmann, Jr., the assistant of Myron C. Taylor, President Roosevelt's personal representative at the Vatican.[53]

Many of the Jewish and Christian leaders seeking the help of the Vatican conveyed their pleas for the Pope to speak out against the Nazi war against the Jews via the nuncios. However, on the whole, the record of the nuncios, who conscientiously forwarded their reports about the plight of the Jews, was not much better than that of the Secretary of State or the Sovereign Pontiff. While many of those assigned to countries in the German sphere of influence expressed concern over some components of the anti-Jewish laws, especially those that impacted on the rights of converts and Christians of Jewish origin, they were generally passive over the other aspects of these laws. Some of them even felt that these laws were in fact beneficial by curtailing Jewish influence considered harmful to Christian society. As Reverend John F. Morley, the noted Catholic scholar, emphasized, "these diplomats viewed the Jewish Badge, and regulations affecting Jewish professions, commerce, and education, as having merit in that they restrained Jewish activity in those areas."[54] Clearly, the nuncios had found that the anti-Jewish laws were in accord with the moral principles of justice and charity.

Some of the nuncios did make considerable efforts on behalf of Jews subjected to deportation. However, these proved useless not only because they were exclusively diplomatic—like their superiors at the Vatican, these nuncios did not speak up publicly—but also because of the single-mindedness with which the Nazis and their accomplices all over Europe were committed to the implementation of the Final Solution program. The issue, as Reverend Morley correctly put it, is not whether the efforts of the nuncios failed to prevent the deportations, but

> ... whether these men used the full weight of their diplomatic positions as representatives of the great moral and religious power that the Holy See claimed to be, in their efforts on behalf of the Jews. One must sadly conclude that they did not. While highly active in defense of Church rights, their involvement in the Jewish problem was tangential at best, and minimal at worst. By lack of total response to the Jews in their hour of greatest needs, the nuncios failed to live up to the high calling that they proclaimed for themselves.[55]

Basically the same attitude of minimal involvement characterized the position of the Secretary of State. The responsibility of Luigi Cardinal Maglione is even greater because he was in charge of papal diplomacy. The nuncios forwarded their diplomatic communications to, and received their instructions directly from, him. The Secretary of State was one of the most well-informed individuals about the great catastrophe that confronted the Jews and the other oppressed people in Nazi-dominated Europe. In addition to receiving reports from the nuncios, he was besieged by appeals from many Jewish and Christian spokesmen for the oppressed, including several prominent Polish Catholics. A voice of indignation was heard even within the walls of the Vatican. In April 1943, Monsignor Domenico Tardini, the Under-secretary of State, intimated in a memorandum that the Vatican had the right to intervene diplomatically for humanitarian purposes. He described the German treatment of the Jews as "an offense not only against justice and charity, but also against humanity." The Secretary of State, however, remained unmoved. While he manifested concern for the baptized Jews threatened with deportation and occasionally even intervened on behalf of some individual Jews, he was not particularly concerned with the suffering of the Jewish people as a whole. An ardent anti-Zionist,[56] Cardinal Maglione was clearly more interested in the preservation of good relations with Nazi Germany and the other states than in using the power and prestige of the Vatican on behalf of the oppressed.

The Silence of Pope Pius XII

The political-ecclesiastical relationship between the Secretary of State and Pope Pius XII was both very close and harmonious. "There is no doubt," Reverend Morley concluded, "that the decisions of Maglione and the instructions he gave to the nuncios were the result of the leadership and orders of the Pope."[57] Like his subordinates, Pope Pius XII was fully and accurately informed about the Nazis' war against the Jews. Acting in tandem with his Secretary of State, he consistently refused to take a public stand to condemn it. The Jewish leaders of the free world, including those associated with the World Jewish Congress, made numerous efforts to induce him to speak out against the exterminations and to threaten Hitler and those actively engaged in the drive with excommunication.[58] Similar appeals were also made by Western leaders. In July 1942, Harold H. Tittmann, Jr., reminded the Vatican that its silence was "endangering its moral prestige and is undermining faith both in the Church and in the Holy Father himself."[59] Shortly after the Allies issued their declaration on the extermination of the Jews on December 17, 1942,[60] Tittmann again approached the Vatican, requesting that it too issue a similar denunciation. His request was rebuffed, the Secretary of State insisting on the Vatican's need to maintain its strict neutrality.[61]

The Vatican adopted a posture of neutrality even when the Jews of Rome were being rounded up for deportation on October 16-17, 1943. To the great relief of the Germans, the Pope refused to allow himself "to be drawn into any demonstrative statement against the deportation of the Jews." Though the measure against the Roman Jews clearly demonstrated to the Vatican just what had happened elsewhere in Nazi-dominated Europe, the Pope refused to break his silence, as he did not want "to say anything that the German people might consider an act of hostility during a terrible war."[62] On the other hand, it was with the Pope's knowledge and approval that more than 4,000 Jews were given refuge in various monasteries and houses of religious orders in Rome.

The Jewish leaders of the free world tried to persuade prominent Catholic ecclesiastical and political figures to intercede with the Pope to end his silence. They wanted the Pontiff to take a public stand condemning the exterminations or threatening the Nazi leaders with excommunication. Their efforts were generally of no avail. Some of the Catholic dignitaries, including Edouard Theunis, the former Prime Minister of Belgium, refused to use their influence, arguing that "His Holiness had serious reasons for not making his stand public."[63] Reportedly, only one Catholic of world renown approached by the Jewish leaders had the courage to condemn the Pope's silence. He was Jacques Maritain, the noted French philosopher-theologian, then living in exile in the United States.[64] Eugene Cardinal Tisserant, a Vatican official, expressed his frustrations over the Pope's attitude in a note to Emmanuel Cardinal Suhard, the Archbishop of Paris. Writing soon after the capitulation of France in June 1940, Cardinal Tisserant asserted that "our superiors do not want to understand the real nature of this conflict." Having failed to persuade the Pope to issue an encyclical "on the duty of the individual to follow the dictates of his conscience rather than blindly execute all orders, no matter how criminal," Cardinal Tisserant revealed his "fear that history will reproach the Holy See with having practiced a policy of selfish convenience and not much else."[65] This historical reproach found the most influential expression after the war in Rolf Hochhuth's "The Deputy" (*Der Stellvertreter*), the controversial play dealing with the failure of Pope Pius XII publicly to condemn the Nazis' destruction of the Jews.

Explanations for the Pope's Silence

The Vatican's standard response to the numerous appeals by Jewish and other groups was "the Holy See will do what it can."[66] The possible reasons for the Pope's silence are complex and not totally verifiable. According to some scholars, the Pontiff failed to speak out against the exterminations because of his "predilection for Germany." The Pope's warmth for the German people, of which more than 20 million were Catholic, and his undisguised appreciation of German culture can perhaps be traced to his twelve years of service in Germany as papal nuncio. Others explain his silence to his fear of and opposition to both Bolshevism and liberalism.[67] The Vatican's abhorrence of Bolshevism was understandable; its leaders made no secret of their contempt for it. The Pope, according to Father Robert Leiber, one of his secretaries, "always looked upon Russian Bolshevism as more dangerous than German National Socialism." Following Italy's extrication from the war in the late summer of 1943, Cardinal Maglione echoed this position by declaring that "the fate of Europe depends on the victorious resistance by Germany on the Russian front."[68] Clearly, the Vatican leaders, like other arch-conservatives the world over, had believed that a reconciliation between Nazi Germany and the Western Allies and the consequent establishment of a common front against the USSR would be in the best interests of the world, including the protection of Christian civilization from the dangers of Bolshevism.[69]

According to many defenders of the Pope at the time, he abhorred the crimes of the Nazis but felt he could not condemn the massacre of the Jews without deploring the mass killing of other groups, or single out the Germans without condemning the Soviets.[70] Others argued that the Pope did not want to risk the allegiance of the German Catholics, many of whom were in the forefront of the struggle against Bolshevism, or to jeopardize the neutrality of the Vatican. Still others believed that the Pontiff adopted a low profile on the Jewish question because he, like many another Church leader in Europe, believed that all his previous diplomatic efforts had been basically futile. The most frequently offered explanation by the Vatican itself was that the Pontiff's policy of public silence on the plight of the Jews was calculated to avoid endangering its quiet diplomacy on their behalf.[71] The shortcoming of this position at the time the Jews were already being massacred was summarized by Guenter Lewy as follows:

> A public denunciation of the mass murders by Pius XII, broadcast widely over the Vatican radio and read from the pulpits by the bishops, would have revealed to Jews and Christians alike what deportation to the East entailed. The Pope would have been believed, whereas the broadcasts of the Allies were often shrugged off as war propaganda. Many of the deportees, who accepted the assurances of the Germans that they were merely being resettled, might thus have been warned and given an impetus to escape. Many more Christians might have helped and sheltered Jews, and many more lives might have been saved.[72]

While the threat of excommunication most probably would not have deterred the ultra-radicals from pursuing their sinister designs, it might have had some influence on the many Catholics (and other Christians) all over Europe who were actively involved in the implementation of the Final Solution.

The Pope remained adamant even during the early part of 1944, when an Allied victory was clearly on the horizon. By that time the Nazis and their accomplices had already completed much of their Final Solution. The close to 800,000 Jews of Hungary constituted the last relatively intact Jewish community. Almost immediately after the German occupation of Hungary on March 19, the Pope was virtually bombarded by appeals for help, but to no avail. In response to an appeal advanced on behalf of Hungarian Jewry by a delegation that included the Chief Rabbi of Rome, the Pope reportedly bypassed the positive steps suggested by the delegation, stating only that he "would pray" for the victims.[73]

The Pope's first direct involvement came late in June 1944, when the Soviet forces were fast approaching Romania and the Western Allies were already firmly established in Normandy—at just about the same time that the Swiss and Swedish press detailed the realities of the Nazis' war against the Jews, based largely on the reports by two escapees from Auschwitz.[74] The Vatican reportedly was among the first to have received a copy of these reports at the end of April 1944.[75] Although the authenticity of these reports was fully corroborated, as were its ominous implications for Hungarian Jewry, the Vatican failed to react until late in June.[76]

But even at this late hour of the Final Solution, the Pope failed to take a public stand. He adamantly refused to heed the pleas coming from many quarters that he appeal directly to the Hungarian people, two-thirds of whom were Catholic. The Pontiff refused to intervene on behalf of Hungarian Jewry even after Isaac Herzog and Ben-Zion Meir Uziel, the Chief Rabbis of Palestine, alerted about the speed and magnitude of the Final Solution in Hungary, contacted him via the Apostolic Delegate's office in Cairo on May 22, 1944, i.e., five days after the initiation of the mass deportations. Subjected to relentless pressure, the Pope finally decided to forward a discreet diplomatic appeal to Miklós Horthy, the Regent of Hungary, pleading for his intervention in behalf of the "unfortunate people" who had "peacefully endured" much suffering "on account of their national or racial origin."[77] In contrast to the almost concurrent appeals by President Roosevelt and King Gustav of Sweden, the Pope was reluctant even at this time to identify the persecuted Jews by name. While the Regent of Hungary was clearly influenced by the appeals, it was the rapidly changing military situation that induced him finally to act. But by the time he halted the deportations early in July 1944, Hungary was (with the notable exception of Budapest) already *Judenrein*.

The wartime attitude of Pope Pius XII can also be illustrated by his refusal to meet with Chief Rabbi Isaac Herzog. The Chief Rabbi's request for an audience with the Pope was subjected to dilatory tactics by the Vatican.[78] On September 5, the Chief Rabbi was invited to meet instead with Monsignor Hughes, the Apostolic Delegate to Cairo, who offered the standard rationalizations for the Pope's refusal to see him. He politely also rejected the Chief Rabbi's plea that the Pope "make a public appeal to the Hungarian people and call on them to place obstacles in the way of the deportation," arguing that such an appeal "may drive the Germans to liquidate the rest of the Hungarian Jews."[79] It would seem that Monsignor Hughes was as uninformed about the political-military realities in Hungary at the time as the Chief Rabbi was: the Germans were in full retreat and the Hungarian leaders were eager to salvage as much of their national patrimony and honor as possible. The Chief Rabbi, for his part, revealed considerable naïveté about the status of the remnant of Hungarian Jewry and, especially, the character of the Hungarian Christian church leaders.[80] The attitude of these leaders generally paralleled that of Angelo Rotta, the Papal Nuncio in Budapest.[81] They approved of most of the anti-Jewish laws, objecting only to their racial component that affected Church interests, and intervened almost exclusively in behalf of converts and non-Aryan Christians.

In summary, Pope Pius XII was concerned primarily with the interests of the Vatican, including the maintenance of good relations with foreign countries. Reflecting his experiences as nuncio in Germany, he felt a special affection for Germany and the German people. Although eager to maintain the Vatican's posture of strict neutrality, his policies and diplomatic maneuvers revealed an understandable fear of both Bolshevism and the Soviet Union. Clearly, like the Catholics in Germany and elsewhere, he was less fearful of Nazism and fascism than of communism, with which the Jews were linked by anti-Semitic propaganda.[82] Like most other leaders of the Christian churches, consequently, the Pope was almost oblivious to the anti-Jewish measures that had been adopted in Nazi-dominated Europe, expressing concern almost exclusively in behalf of the converts and non-Aryan Christians. The currently available historical evidence reveals that he failed to confront the evils that threatened the Jewish people in Christian Europe. As Reverend Morley aptly concluded:

Vatican diplomacy failed the Jews during the Holocaust by not doing all that it was possible for it to do on their behalf. It also failed itself because in neglecting the needs of the Jews, and pursuing a goal of reserve rather than humanitarian concern, it betrayed the ideals that it had set for itself. The nuncios, the secretary of state, and, most of all, the Pope share the responsibility for this dual failure.[83]

Toward Reconciliation and Harmony

Clearly, the Vatican document on the Holocaust, like the *Nostra Aetate* Declaration, is less than thorough in its treatment of past wrongs. The vital interests of the Church apparently required that it:

- Deflect all responsibility for what had happened to the Jewish people during the long history of Christianity by placing exclusive blame on the failures of her sons and daughters;

- Protect the authority of the Pontiffs;

- Clearly differentiate Christian anti-Judaism from Nazi neopagan anti-Semitism, identifying the latter as both anti-Jewish and anti-Christian and exclusively responsible for the Holocaust.

The weaknesses of the 1965 and 1998 documents are largely balanced by a very positive orientation toward the future. As Rabbi A. James Rudin, Director of the American Jewish Committee's Interreligious Affairs Department, correctly observed, "there have been more positive encounters [between Jews and Christians] since 1965 than there were in the first 1900 years of the Church." Mutual suspicions between Catholics and Jews have broken down; mutual stereotypes have been replaced by civilized discourse and dialogue. At a February 15, 1985 meeting with some American Jewish leaders, Pope John Paul II asserted that "relationships between Jews and Christians have radically improved.... Where there was ignorance and...prejudice...there is now growing mutual knowledge, appreciation and respect."[84]

The American Catholic bishops were among the first to advance the cause of interreligious reconciliation and harmony. Even before the issuance of *Nostra Aetate*, the American bishops had decided to establish a commission in the National Conference of Catholic Bishops to promote Catholic-Jewish understanding. In 1967, they established an Office on Catholic-Jewish Relations, which promptly issued *Guidelines for Catholic-Jewish Relations*. These preceded and presumably served as model for the *Guidelines for Implementing Nostra Aetate, No. 4*, which the Vatican issued on January 3, 1975.[85] Designed to further fellowship between Christians and Jews, the Vatican *Guidelines* provide directives for furthering dialogues, placing Jews in a favorable light in liturgy, and focusing on the common heritage in teaching and education.

The changes introduced by the American bishops, and subsequently by the Vatican, resulted in the purging of education and liturgy of anti-Jewish references.[86] The bishops urged all those involved in education, whether in the seminary, the school or the pulpit, not only to avoid any presentation that might disparage Jews and Judaism but also, in accord with *Nostra Aetate*, to emphasize those aspects of the faith which bear witness to Catholicism's spiritual ties with the Jews. With respect to the Holocaust, the American bishops reaffirmed the conclusions of the Vatican, deploring the suffering of the Jews and condemning all forms of anti-Semitism.[87]

Similar positions were taken by Catholic bishops in many other parts of the Christian world. On the occasion of the fiftieth anniversary of the Holocaust in Hungary, for example, the Hungarian Catholic Bishops' Conference and the Ecumenical Council of the Churches of Hungary[88] issued a joint declaration stating, among other things:

> We believe that the murder of hundreds of thousands of people merely because of their origin was the greatest shame of the twentieth century.... On the occasion of this anniversary, we must state that responsibility for this tragedy lies not only with the representatives of this irrational evil, but also with those who considered themselves members of our churches and failed to raise their voices against the mass humiliation, deportation, and murder of their Jewish fellowmen whether out of fear, cowardice, or opportunism. For these omissions during the catastrophe that took place fifty years ago, we ask forgiveness before God.[89]

Although the declaration failed to identify the responsibility of the Christian Churches for the anti-Semitic climate that prevailed during the long history of Hungary in general and the 1919-1944 period in particular, it represents a long step forward toward coming to grips with the Holocaust in that country.

The German Catholic bishops issued a similar admission of guilt on January 27, 1995. In a statement issued on the occasion of the fiftieth anniversary of the liberation of Auschwitz, the German bishops deplored the failure of Catholics to act against Nazism and to speak out against the crimes committed against Jews and Judaism, emphasizing that they consequently bore a special responsibility to fight against anti-Semitism.[90] The anniversary also served as an occasion for the issuance of a Declaration by the Polish Episcopate Commission's for Dialogue with Judaism. While emphasizing the common suffering of Jews and Poles at the hands of the Nazis, the Declaration repeated, among other things, the Polish Bishops' Pastoral Letter of January 20,

1991, deploring the behavior of those Christians who had remained indifferent to the tragedy of the Jews and mourning "the fact that there were also those among Catholics who in some way had contributed to the death of Jews." Instead of an apology, the Declaration merely stated: "They will forever remain a remorse in the social dimension."[91]

The anniversary of the liberation of Auschwitz was also commemorated by American Catholics. In his statement of January 27, 1995, Archbishop Oscar Lipscomb of Mobile, Alabama, Chairman of the U.S. Bishops' Committee for Ecumenical and Interreligious Affairs, emphasized the need of repentance and a "resolve to build a world where never again will such evil be possible." While correctly absolving Americans of any personal guilt for what the Nazis had done, the statement acknowledged "a real sense of responsibility for what fellow members in the community of the baptized did not do to save lives." It also deplored America's wartime immigration policies by pointing out that "the bitter enforcement of the draconian immigration laws of the period...kept this country from becoming the asylum for Jews...."[92]

On September 30, 1997, the French Catholic Church issued a remarkable statement in Drancy, the Paris suburb from which tens of thousands of Jews had been deported to Auschwitz during the Vichy era. Issued by Archbishop Olivier de Barranger, the statement declared *inter alia*:

> It is important to admit the primary role, if not direct, then indirect, played by the constantly repeated anti-Jewish stereotypes wrongly perpetuated among Christians in the historical process that led to the Holocaust.
>
> In the face of the persecution of Jews, especially the multi-faceted anti-Semitic laws passed by Vichy, silence was the rule, and words in favor of the victims the exception.
>
> Today we confess that silence was a mistake. We beg for the pardon of God, and we ask the Jewish people to hear this word of repentance. We beg God's forgiveness and ask the Jewish people to hear our words of repentance.[93]

Similar documents were issued by many other national Catholic hierarchies, including those of Italy, the Netherlands, and Switzerland.[94]

It is clear that most of the statements issued by national Catholic episcopates were in response to the *Nostra Aetate* Declaration and the Vatican Guidelines relating to its implementation. A decisive role was also played by the many declarations Pope John Paul II has made during his long pontificate on the need to fight the scourge of racism and anti-Semitism and on the desirability to advance Catholic-Jewish relations.

Clearly, the *We Remember* document fails to provide a full and unvarnished account of the Vatican's role during the Nazi era in general or the silence of Pope Pius XII during the Holocaust in particular. Reflecting the Vatican's institutional interests, the document, devoted to the remembering the Shoah, also found it necessary to universalize it by recalling the great human tragedies of the nineteenth and twentieth centuries, including the massacre of the Armenians, the "tragedies which have occurred in America, Africa, and the Balkans...the millions of victims of totalitarian ideology in the Soviet Union, China, Cambodia...and the drama of the Middle East." On the whole, the Vatican document reflects the many pronouncements by Pope John Paul II by failing to emphatically admit the institutional guilt of the Church and by staunchly defending the wartime position of Pope Pius XII.[95] These issues—and many others that continue to divide Jews and Catholics as well as the Vatican and the State of Israel[96]—will undoubtedly continue to be the subject of Catholic-Jewish dialogues for many years to come. It is fair to assume that the debate will be brought to a successful conclusion only after the Vatican permits full and unhindered access to all its archives.[97] Unfortunately, the Vatican's position in this regard is not very encouraging.[98]

The shortcomings notwithstanding, it is absolutely clear that *Nostra Aetate* and the *We Remember* documents of the Vatican and the clear and unambiguous statements issued by Pope John Paul II and many national episcopates have gone a long way in healing Catholic-Jewish relations and in laying the foundation for the eventual triumph of the spirit of tolerance and mutual respect.

NOTES

1. Under preparation for 11 years, the 14-page document was completed by the Vatican's Commission for Religious Relations With the Jews at the direction of Pope John Paul II. The document was released under the signature of Edward Idris Cardinal Cassidy, the Australian-born President of the Commission, the Most Reverend Pierre Duprey, Vice President, and the Reverend Remi Hoeckman, serving as secretary. For text, see Appendix A. See also *Catholics Remember the Holocaust* (Washington, DC: United States Catholic Conference, 1998), pp. 47-56.

The Pope had promised to issue a Holocaust-related document during a 1987 meeting with American Jewish leaders in Miami. At that meeting. the Jewish leaders had suggested the issuance of an encyclical.

2. The First Vatican Council was held in 1869. Dedicated to the preservation of the traditional prerogatives of the Church, it promulgated a "Syllabus of Errors" in which it condemned the modern conceptions of religious toleration, socialism, the theory of evolution, and political liberalism.

3. After three years of deliberations, the Second Vatican Council, the conclave of the world's Catholic bishops, adopted the *Nostra Aetate* document during the papacy of Paul VI on October 28, 1965. (Pope John XXIII died in 1963.) For text, see Appendix B. On the antecedents of *Nostra Aetate*, see also Geoffrey Wigoder, *Jewish-Christian Relations Since the Second World War* (Manchester: Manchester University Press, 1988), and Johannes Cardinal Willebrands, *Church and the Jewish People* (New York: Paulist Press, 1992).

4. On June 25, 1987, for example, the leaders of the American Jewish Congress published an open letter in *The New York Times*, requesting an explanation for the Pope's decision to grant an audience to Kurt Waldheim, the controversial President of Austria, who had lied about his wartime activities as a Wehrmacht officer. At a ceremonial meeting with Jewish organizational leaders in Miami in October 1987, Pope John Paul II expressed the belief that Pope Pius XII would be vindicated by history. Angered, the Jewish leaders assumed that the statement was designed to further the rehabilitation of the controversial wartime Pontiff.

5. The Pope made these remarks during an address to Catholic, Protestant, and Orthodox scholars who were attending a symposium in Rome on "The Roots of Anti-Judaism in the Christian Milieu" sponsored by the Historical-Theological Commission of the Committee for the Great Jubilee of the Year 2000.

6. In the course of time, Pope John Paul II also apologized for the persecution of Protestants and the crimes of the Crusaders; asked forgiveness for the abuses of proselytizing around the world; voiced regret over the Church's repression of Galileo; and condemned its silence on the murderous activities of the Mafia in Italy. Celestine Bohlen, "The Pope's in a Confessional, and Jews Are Listening," *The New York Times*, November 30, 1997.

7. In differentiating between the Church and its members, many Catholic theologians look upon the Church as "the bride of Christ, the heavenly Jerusalem, holy and sinless." See, for example, the explanation by Edward Idris Cardinal Cassidy in *Perspectives on We Remember: A Reflection on the Shoah* (New York: The American Jewish Committee, July 1998), p. 10.

8. The quote is from the Pope's address to the October 1997 Vatican Symposium on "The Christian Roots of Anti-Judaism." The original text was published in *L'Osservatore Romano*, November 1, 1997, p. 6.

9. For a perceptive and well-documented account of the connection between Christian anti-Semitism and the Holocaust, see Hyam Maccoby's piece in this volume.

10. The Vatican document does not refer to such major anti-Jewish drives as the Crusades, the Fourth Lateran Council of 1215 that required distinctive clothing for Jews, the establishment of the Rome ghetto under the Papal Encyclical of 1555, or the

expulsion of the Jews from the Papal States by Pope Pius V in 1569. See in this context the comments by Morton S. Kaplan, chairman of the Interreligious Affairs Commission of the American Jewish Committee, in *Perspectives on We Remember: A Reflection on the Shoah, op. cit.,* pp. 15-30.

11. Jules Isaac, *Jésus et Israël* (Paris: Pasquelle Editeurs, 1959), p. 508.

12. John T. Pawlikowski, "The Vatican and the Holocaust: Putting *We Remember* in Context," *Dimensions,* Vol. 12, No. 2, p. 15.

13. See, for example, "The Survivors of the Holocaust Respond to the Vatican's Document 'We Remember: A Reflection on the Shoah (Holocaust)'," *The Jewish Week,* May 15, 1998.

14. Provost Lichtenberg was arrested on October 23, 1941—a week after the mass deportations from Germany began. He denounced the deportations as "irreconcilable with Christian moral law," and requested permission to accompany the deportees as their spiritual advisor. Imprisoned for two years, he was rearrested by the Gestapo in October 1943. He died on November 5, en route to Dachau. Guenter Lewy, *The Catholic Church and Nazi Germany* (New York: McGraw Hill, 1964), p. 293. See also Saul Friedländer, *Pius XII and the Third Reich* (New York: Alfred A. Knopf, 1966), p. 91.

15. Klaus Scholder, *A Requiem for Hitler* (Philadelphia: Trinity Press International, 1989), pp. 164-67. The Vatican document emphasized that Cardinals Bertram, Faulhaber and some other Catholic Church leaders issued pastoral letters in February and March 1931 condemning National Socialism. Cardinal Faulhaber is also cited for his 1933 Advent sermons, rejecting anti-Semitic propaganda. For details on Cardinal Faulhaber, see Gordon C. Zahn, *German Catholics and Hitler's Wars* (New York: Sheed and Ward, 1962), chapter 8. For some additional details on Cardinal Bertram's requiem, see below.

16. The principal founder and theorist of the movement was Father Franziskus Stratmann. At the height of its popularity, the movement had 40,000 members. It was dissolved by the Nazis on July 1, 1933. Zahn, pp. 1, 5.

17. Article 24 of the National Socialist Workers' Party program, which was adopted on February 20, 1920, demanded, among other things, "liberty for all religious denominations in the state, so far as they are not a danger to it and do not militate against the morality and the moral sense of the Germanic race"—provisions of liberty and morality to be determined by the Nazis themselves.

18. Lewy, p. 271.

19. The declaration, made public on March 28, 1933, was largely based on Bishop Bertram's draft. *Ibid.,* pp. 39-40.

20. For details on the Fulda Bishops' Conference, see *ibid.,* pp. 94ff.

21. Even before the Nazi acquisition of power, the Holy See concluded concordats with Bavaria (1924), Prussia (1929), and Baden (1932), the three states in which most of the German Catholics lived. For details on the Concordat with the Third Reich, see *ibid.,* pp. 57-94.

22. Zahn, pp. 119-20. Interestingly, Cardinal Gröber was also a member of the German Catholic Peace Union during the Weimar republic. For further details, see *ibid.,* chapter 9. See also Lewy, pp. 45-46.

23. *Ibid.,* p. 277. Although not mentioned by name, Cardinal Gröber is identified in the Vatican document of March 16, 1998, as a positive figure, emphasizing the pastoral letter he and other Catholic ecclesiastical leaders published in 1931 condemning National Socialism.

24. *Ibid.,* p. 279.

25. The meeting was attended by Bishop Berning and Monsignor Steinmann. *Ibid.,* pp. 50-51.

26. Bishop Bertram tried to blunt the effect of the encyclical by ruling that the critical passages were not to be read out, contending that they were meant only for the leaders rather than the masses of believers. Scholder, p. 159.

27. Lewy, pp. 156-57. See also Zahn, pp. 76-77.

28. "With Burning Anxiety," *The New Republic*, April 6, 1998. See also Lewy, p. 158, and Georges Passelecq and Bernard Suchecky, *The Hidden Encyclical of Pius XI* (New York: Harcourt Brace, 1997).

29. John F. Morley, *Vatican Diplomacy and the Jews During the Holocaust, 1939-1943* (New York: Ktav, 1980), p. 196.

30. This was as true of Michael Cardinal Faulhaber, who, as the Vatican statement on the Holocaust correctly noted in 1933 rejected the Nazis' anti-Semitic program, as of Franz Josef Rarkowski, the Catholic Military Bishop, who enthusiastically supported Hitler's regime and wars. For details on Faulhaber, Rarkowski, see *Scholder*, chapters 8 and 10, respectively. See also Ernst Christian Helmreich, *The German Churches under Hitler: Background, Struggle, and Epilogue* (Detroit: Wayne State University Press, 1979).

31. Zahn, p. 137. According to Zahn's finding, only seven German Catholics dared to refuse military service; six of these were executed, the seventh was placed into a military mental institution. *Ibid.*, p. 54.

32. *Ibid.*, pp. 202-3

33. In his Reichstag speech of January 30, 1939, Hitler declared: "If international Jewry should succeed, in Europe or elsewhere, in precipitating nations into a world war, the result will not be the Bolshevization of Europe and a victory for Judaism, but the extermination of the Jewish race."

34. By the end of 1942, the Nazis had deported more than 100,000 German Jews.

35. For details on their sources of information, see Lewy, pp. 287-88.

36. In addition to offering daily prayers for German Jews, Father Lichtenberg also guided the work of the Special Relief of the Diocese of Berlin (*Hilfswerk beim Ordinariat Berlin*). For some details, see Michael Phayer, "The Catholic Resistance Circle in Berlin and German Catholic Bishops during the Holocaust," *Holocaust and Genocide Studies*, Vol. 7, No. 2, Fall 1993, P. 218. See also endnote 14.

37. After Canon Lichtenberg's arrest by the Gestapo in October 1941, Margarete Sommer took over the leadership of the Special Relief office and emerged, with the support of Konrad Cardinal Preysing of Berlin, as the German episcopacy's chief adviser on Jewish affairs. She worked closely with Gertrud Luckner in keeping the German Catholic bishops informed about the Nazis' drive against the Jews. Luckner was imprisoned by the Gestapo in 1943. *Ibid.*, pp. 216

38. Addressing a conference of priests at Fulda in 1943, Father Delp decried the failure of the Church to stand up for human dignity. At a gathering of Bavarian churchmen in October 1943, he also expressed his anxiety over the murder of Jews and Poles. Lewy, p. 307.

39. *Ibid.*, pp. 292-93.

40. For additional documentation relating to the German Catholic bishops' awareness of the Final Solution, see Phayer, *op. cit.* See also Frank M. Buscher and Michael Phayer, "German Catholic Bishops and the Holocaust, 1940-1952," *German Studies Review*, October 1988.

41. Scholder, p. 166.

42. Although completed before the death of Pius XI, its issuance was blocked. According to some scholars, the failure to issue the encyclical constituted "one of the greatest and most tragically missed opportunities of history." In their view, the encyclical might have restrained the Nazis from implementing the Final Solution program. Michael R. Marrus, a highly respected scholar of the Holocaust, on the other hand, demonstrated that the draft encyclical appeared "much more like a repetition of conventional wisdom of the Church on antisemitism than a call to arms against anti-Semitic forces in Germany and Italy." See his "The Vatican on Racism and Antisemitism, 1938-39. A New Look at a Might-Have-Been," *Holocaust and Genocide Studies,* Vol. 7, No. 3, Winter 1997, pp. 378-95.

43. In some countries, including Croatia and Slovakia, leading figures of the Catholic Church were in the forefront of the anti-Jewish measures. In Hungary, the Christian church leaders publicly supported almost all of the anti-Jewish laws prior to the country's occupation by the Germans on March 19, 1944.

44. On September 7, 1945, Joseph Nathan, representing the Italian Hebrew Commission, thanked the Pope for his help during the war. In his highly critical essay on the wartime position of Pope Pius XII, Aryeh L. Kubovy (formerly Leon A. Kubowitzki), the secretary of the World Jewish Congress during and after the war, mentions his expressions of thanks on behalf of the Congress and of the Union of Italian Jewish Communities during his interview with the Pope on September 21, 1945, as follows: "I was asked by my organization during my stay in Rome to convey to you the thanks of our communities for the things the Church has attempted to do and has done on behalf of our persecuted people." Kubovy left a donation of two million lire ($20,000) for the Pope's charities "as a nominal participation in the expenses incurred by the Vatican by its assistance to the Jews," See his "The Silence of Pope Pius XII and the Beginnings of the 'Jewish Document'," in *Yad Vashem Studies,* Vol. 6, 1967 pp. 21, 23. Thanks were also conveyed to the Pope by Chief Rabbi Isaac Herzog of Palestine via Monsignor Hughes, the Apostolic Delegate to Cairo, despite the fact that his pleas on behalf of the Jews were left basically unheeded. Friedländer, pp. 230, 233.

45. In citing the exaggerated figure, the Vatican, like many other Catholic organizations, apparently relied on the "proof" provided by Pinchas Lapide, a Canadian-born journalist and former Israeli official. Without providing any empirical documentation, Lapide claimed that the Catholic Church had been instrumental in saving close to 860,000 Jewish lives. See his *Three Popes and the Jews* (New York: Hawthorne, 1967). The exaggerated figure clearly includes the close to 100,000 Jews of Budapest whose deportation was halted by Miklós Horthy, the Hungarian head of state, on July 7, 1944. Acting primarily in response to the worsening military situation, Horthy's decision followed shortly after Pope Pius XII—along with President Roosevelt, and King Gustav of Sweden—beseeched him to halt the anti-Jewish drive. Credit for the rescue of these Jews is claimed not only by the former Hungarian head of state and the Vatican, but also by the Raoul Wallenberg myth-makers, and even the Nazis. Randolph L. Braham, *The Politics of Genocide. The Holocaust in Hungary* (New York: Columbia University Press, 1994), p. 939, footnote 152.

46. Edith Stein was later known as Sister Teresia Benedicta a Cruce of the Order of the Carmelites. In August 1942, she was arrested by the Gestapo at a Dutch monastery, where she had sought refuge, and deported to Auschwitz. Beatified in 1987, she was canonized in 1998 by Pope Paul II—an act many Jews identified as an attempt to Christianize or universalize the Holocaust, emphasizing that she was murdered by the Nazis for having been Jewish not Christian. Alessandra Stanley, " A Jew's Odyssey From Catholic Nun to Saint," *The New York Times,* October 11, 1998. See also James Carroll, "The Saint and the Holocaust," *The New Yorker,* June 7, 1999, pp. 52-57.

47. For details consult Morley. See also Friedländer.

48. The nuncios are in effect envoys of the Vatican, assigned to protect the interests of the Church and to serve as liaison between the particular governments and the Holy See.

49. Paul Hofmann, "Pius Knew in 1941 of Drive on Jews," *The New York Times,* April 27, 1974. On Orsenigo's position, especially in connection with Konrad Cardinal Preysing's attempt to pressure the Pope to intervene on behalf of the Jews, see Phayer, "The Catholic Resistance Circle in Berlin...," pp. 224ff.

50. Paul Hofmann, "The Vatican Knew of Nazi Pogroms, Its Records Show," *The New York Times,* April 5, 1973.

51. For some additional details about the nuncios' reports to the Vatican, see Morley, pp. 198-99, 202-3.

52. For Gerstein's statement of April 26, 1945, see PS-1553. See also Friedländer, pp. 125-29.

53. Nora Levin, *The Holocaust* (New York: Thomas Y. Crowell, 1968), pp. 686-87.

54. Morley, p. 198.

55. *Ibid.*, p. 200.

56. Like many others in the Church, including Under-Secretary Tardini and Archbishop Angelo Roncalli, the Apostolic Delegate in Ankara, Cardinal Maglione argued against the notion of a Jewish homeland. *Ibid.*, p. 206.

57. *Ibid.*, p. 207.

58. Kubovy, p. 11. See also appeals by the British Section of the World Jewish Congress of June 26 and October 14, 1944, in behalf of Hungarian Jewry, in *Public Records Office* (PRO), London, Fo.371/42807, p. 32, and Fo.371/42820, p. 22.

59. *Foreign Relations of the United States, Diplomatic Papers, 1942.* Vol. 3. *Europe.* (Washington: Government Printing Office, 1961), pp. 776-77. For additional documents on the subject, see section titled "Vatican. Efforts of the United States and Other Governments to Have the Pope Protest Publicly Against Nazi Atrocities in German Occupied Areas," *ibid.,* pp. 772-80. See also Levin, *The Holocaust,* p. 686.

60. This declaration by the Allies was the first to define the extermination of the Jews as a crime. For some details on the declaration, see Braham, pp. 1248-49.

61. Lewy, p. 299.

62. Report of Ernst von Weizsäcker, former Secretary of State in the German Foreign Office and then German Ambassador to the Holy See, dated October 28, 1943. Alvin Shuster, "Vatican Releases '43 Documents on Handling of Jewish Problems," *The New York Times,* January 24, 1976; Raul Hilberg, *The Destruction of the European Jews* (Chicago: Quadrangle, 1961), pp. 429-30. See also Lewy, pp. 300-2, and Robert G. Weisbord and Wallace P. Sillanpoa, *The Chief Rabbi, the Pope, and the Holocaust* (New Brunswick: Transaction Publishers, 1992).

63. Kubovy, p. 11.

64. *Ibid.*

65. Lewy, pp. 306-7.

66. The standard response was usually given by Monsignor Montini on instructions from the Pope. It was revealed in a note attached by Monsignor Montini to a telegram received from an Orthodox Jewish group in December 1942, in which the Pope was requested to intervene in behalf of the Jews of Eastern Europe. Hofmann, "Pius Knew in 1941 of Drive on Jews," cited above.

67. According to Professor John T. Pawlikowski, until the 1940s, Pope Pius XII "was a fervent believer and participant in the century-long struggle of the Catholic Church against the growing power of the liberal political order in Western Europe." See his "The Vatican and the Holocaust," *op. cit.*, p. 16.

68. Friedländer, p. 190, 236; Levin, pp. 692-93; Lewy, p. 305. The view that Pope Pius XII "looked to the National Socialists to 'save' the Church from the Bolshevism menacing Europe" is counteracted by Robert A. Graham in his *The Vatican and Communism in World War II* (San Francisco: Ignatius Press, 1996).

69. For a well-documented account of Pope Pius XII's maneuverings to split the Grand Alliance during the war, and his postwar role in the anti-communist and anti-Soviet drive, see Michael Phayer, "Pope Pius XII, the Holocaust, and the Cold War," *Holocaust and Genocide Studies,* Vol. 12, No. 2, Fall 1998, pp. 223-56.

70. For example, in response to the October 14, 1944 appeal by Alex L. Easterman, the Political Secretary of the British Section of the World Jewish Congress, the Pope refused to make a public appeal, arguing that "if he made a public declaration about the treatment of Jews in Hungary he might have to yield to pressure to issue a similar statement in regard to Russian treatment of Poles and the Baltic populations." See telegram no. 701, dated November 20, 1944, from Sir D. Osborne, the British Minister to the Holy See, to the Foreign Office. PRO, Fo.371/42822, p. 86.

71. John T. Pawlikowski, "The Vatican and the Holocaust," p. 16. This theme was also echoed in the 688-page volume of documents issued by the Vatican early in 1976. See *Le Saint Siège et les victimes de la guerre, janvier 1944 - juillet 1945* (Vatican City: Libreria Editrice Vaticana, 1980) [*Actes et documents du Saint Siège relatif à la Seconde Guerre Mondiale*, Vol. X]. The volume reveals the anti-Zionist bias of the Vatican, many of whose officers, including Cardinal Maglione, openly opposed the establishment of a Jewish state in Palestine. Alvin Shuster, "Vatican Releases '43 Documents on Handling of Jewish Problems."

For a sympathetic evaluation of the Pope's role, see Carlo Falconi, *The Silence of Pius XII* (Boston: Little, Brown, 1970); Robert A. Graham, *Pope Pius XII and the Jews of Hungary in 1944* (New York: The America Press for the United States Catholic Historical Society, 1964), and his *Pius XII's Defense of the Jews and Others: 1944-45* (Milwaukee: Catholic League for Religious and Civil Rights, 1982); Jenö Lévai, *Hungarian Jewry and the Papacy* (London: Sands and Company, 1968); and Anthony Rhodes, *The Vatican in the Age of the Dictators, 1922-1945* (New York: Holt, Rinehart and Winston, 1973). See also *Pius XII and the Holocaust: A Reader* (Milwaukee: Catholic League for Religious and Civil Rights, 1988), and Kenneth L. Woodward, "In Defense of Pius XII," *Newsweek*, March 30, 1998.

72. Lewy, p. 303. See also Friedländer, pp. 103-47, 236-38.

73. The other members of the delegation were Gil Jakov, the chaplain of the Jewish Brigade then stationed near Rome, and Ben Dor, the correspondent of *Davar*. Gil Jakov, "XII. Pius Pápa magatartása a Soáidején" (The Attitude of Pope Pius XII During the Holocaust)," *Uj Kelet* (New East), Tel Aviv, October 9, 1987.

74. The Auschwitz reports were prepared in Zilina, Slovakia, toward the end of April 1944, on the basis of the accounts by Walter Rosenberg (Rudolf Vrba) and Alfred Wetzler, who had escaped from Auschwitz on April 7. For some details, see Braham, pp. 824-32.

75. These were forwarded to the Vatican by Monsignor Giuseppe Burzio, the Nuncio in Bratislava. According to Vatican sources, Monsignor Burzio's copy was sent out only on May 22, 1944, and was not received until October 20. *Le Saint Siège et les victimes de la guerre, janvier 1944 – juillet 1945*, p. 281, note 1. Another copy of the Reports—probably the one sent by Miklós (Moshe) Krausz on June 19, 1944—reached the Vatican via Monsignor Filippo Bernardini, the Apostolic Delegate in Bern, toward the end of June.

76. The Vatican insisted on the verification of the reports. It was only after one its emissaries, Monsignor Mario Martillotti, corroborated the veracity of the reports after interviewing two escapees from Auschwitz, did the Pope decide to appeal to Miklós Horthy, Hungary's head of state. Braham, p. 830.

77. For the text of his telegram of June 25, 1944, see *ibid.,* p. 1219. See also Friedländer, p. 224.

78. These efforts and the apparent resistance by the Vatican were detailed in a July 1944 letter Jacob Herzog, the Chief Rabbi's son and secretary, sent to Isaac Ben-Zvi, a member of the Jewish Agency Executive (and a future President of Israel). For details, see Friedländer, pp. 224-26.

79. *Ibid.*, p. 231.

80. The Chief Rabbi made, among other things, the following suggestion to Monsignor Hughes: "If Hungarian Bishops were to go into the camps and announce publicly that, if deportation of Jews went on, they (the Bishops) would go and die with them. I think it would be difficult for the Germans to continue the deportations." *Ibid.*, p. 233. Clearly, the Chief Rabbi was not informed about the questionable attitude of the various Christian church leaders in Hungary during the Nazi era. For details on their attitude, see Braham, chapter 30 and *passim.*

81. Angelo Rotta, the Apostolic Delegate, was also the dean of the diplomatic corps in Budapest. An extremely able and compassionate man, the Nuncio took the leadership after the German occupation in warning the members of the newly estab-

lished quisling government of Döme Sztójay against any anti-Jewish excesses. On the eve of the deportations on May 15, 1944, the Nuncio delivered a note to the Ministry of Foreign Affairs, requesting the government "not to continue its war against the Jews beyond the limits prescribed by the laws of nature and God's commandments." Although qualified and non-public, the note is of particular importance because, as Saul Friedländer observed, "it was the first official protest against the deportation of Jews made by a representative of the Holy See. Friedländer, p. 218. For the Nuncio's account see his "A budapesti nunciatura diplomáciai akciója a zsidók érdekében" (The Diplomatic Campaign of the Budapest Nunciature in Behalf of the Jews) in Antal Meszlényi, ed., *A magyar katolikus egyhdz és az emberi jogok védelme* (The Hungarian Catholic Church and the Protection of Human Rights) (Budapest: A Szent István Társulat, 1947), pp. 21-30.

82. For further details, see Phayer, "Pope Pius XII, the Holocaust, and the Cold War."

83. Morley, p. 209.

84. A. James Rudin, "Catholics, Jews: 20 Good Years," *The New York Times*, February 23, 1985.

85. The *Guidelines and Suggestions for Implementing the Concillar Declaration "Nostra Aetate" (No. 4)* were issued under the signature of Johannes Cardinal Willebrands and Pierre-Marie de Contenson, President and Secretary, respectively, of the Vatican Commission for Religious Relations with the Jews. For text, see Appendix C.

86. See *Notes on the Correct Way to Present the Jews and Judaism in Preaching and Catechesis in the Roman Catholic Church*, issued by the Vatican's Commission for Religious Relations with the Jews on June 24, 1985. Appendix D.

87. "Pastoral Message: The Church and the Synagogue," *Origins: CNS Documentary Service*, Vol. V, No. 24, 1975.

88. *A Magyar Katolikus Püspöki Konferencia és a Magyarországi Egyházak Okumenikus Tanácsa.*

89. The declaration was issued under the signature of Bishop Csaba Tornyák, secretary of the Hungarian Catholic Bishops' Conference. It was reproduced, among others, in *Magyar Hirlap* (Hungarian Journal), Budapest, November 30, 1994. On October 26, 1992, the Conference issued a declaration condemning anti-Semitism and all forms of racial discrimination. For excerpts from the English version of the 1994 declaration, see *Catholics Remember the Holocaust*, pp. 7-8.

90. For a summary of the statement, see Stephen Kinzer, "German Bishops Cite Catholic 'Denial and Guilt' at Holocaust," *The New York Times,* January 27, 1995. See also *Catholics Remember the Holocaust*, pp. 9-11.

91. *Ibid.*, pp. 12-15. The Declaration was signed on behalf of the Commission by Bishop Stanislav Gadecki. The text is available, among others, in the archives of the American Jewish Committee.

92. "Commemorating the Liberation of Auschwitz," *Origins: CNS Documentary Service*, Vol. 24, No. 34, February 9, 1995. See also *Catholics Remember the Holocaust*, pp. 16-20. Among the many positive comments by American Catholic dignitaries about the Vatican document were those advanced by John Cardinal O'Connor of New York, and William Cardinal Keeler and Eugene Fisher. *Ibid.*, pp. 57-60.

93. *Ibid.*, pp. 31-37. For a summary of the statement, see Roger Cohen, "French Church Issues Apology to Jews on War," *The New York Times*, October 1, 1997. For the complete original text, see "Les évêques de France et le statut des juifs sous le régime de Vichy," *La Documentation Catholique*, No. 2168, October 19, 1997.

94. *Catholics Remember the Holocaust.*, pp. 21-26, 38-40.

95. The Vatican appears to be pursuing quite actively the planned beatification of Pope Pius XII. The beatification effort is directed by Reverend Peter Gumpel, a

Jesuit priest, acting on behalf of the Congregation for the Causes of Saints. See Alessandra Stanley, "Israeli Diplomat Urges Vatican to Delay Beatification of Pius XII," *The New York Times*, November 5, 1998.

96. Among these, to cite only a few, are the role many Catholic clergymen (some of them associated with the Vatican) played in the escape of suspected war criminals, the Vatican's position on the ultimate status of Jerusalem, the appointment of Pierre Mouallem, reportedly a pro-PLO Palestinian, as Archbishop of the mainly Arabic-speaking Melkite Christians in the Galilee, the beatification and subsequent canonization of Edith Stein, and the beatification of Alojzije Cardinal Stepinac, the controversial Archbishop of Zagreb during the pro-Nazi Ustashe era of Croatia.

For details on the Vatican's role in the rescue of suspected war criminals, see Mark Aarons and John Loftus, *Unholy Trinity* (New York: St. Martin's Press, 1991), and Gitta Sereny, *Into That Darkness* (New York: Vintage Books, 1983). See also endnotes 4 and 45.

97. Shortly after the *We Remember* document was issued on March 16, 1998, Edward Cardinal Cassidy proposed the creation of a Jewish-Catholic commission to jointly study 12 published volumes from the Church's secret World War II archives. Like most official documentary collections, it is presumed that the 12 volumes published between 1965 and 1981 under the direction of Vatican-approved scholars, too, contain only carefully selected materials. Under Vatican rules, the wartime archives must remain sealed for another twenty years. However, in September 1998, in a move hailed by many interfaith leaders as a breakthrough, John Cardinal O'Connor, the Roman Catholic Archbishop of New York, called for the Vatican to quickly open its Nazi era archives. *The Jewish Week*, October 9, 1998.

98. In a three-page "Statement by the Holy See About the Accessibility of Its Archives," which was distributed by Father Remi Hoeckman, Secretary of the Vatican's Commission on Relations With the Jews, at the November 1998 International Conference on Holocaust-Era Looted Assets organized by the Washington-based United States Holocaust Memorial Museum, the Vatican declared that "the Holy See alone must be the judge of the pace, timing, and scope of the process of making its archives accessible for research." Eric J. Greenberg, "Vatican to U.S.: No Archives." *The Jewish Week*, December 11, 1998.

3

Reaction of a Catholic Theologian to the Vatican's *We Remember* Document

John F. Morley

Introduction

In discussing a document as important as *We Remember: A Reflection on the Shoah* [WR], there are a number of facts and considerations that must be kept in mind if the purpose and meaning of the statement is to be clearly understood. It should not be surprising, first of all, that it is addressed to Catholics in terms and concepts traditional to the Church and familiar to us. The Pope, in his covering letter released at the same time that WR was published, referred to the millennium, obviously a Christian concept based on the birth of Christ, and the need "...for [the] sons and daughters [of the Church] to purify their hearts through repentance of past errors and infidelities."[1]

Indeed, WR makes this even more precise:

> At the end of this millennium the Catholic Church desires to express her deep sorrow for the failures of her sons and daughters in every age. This is an act of repentance (*teshuva*) since as members of the Church we are linked to the sins as well as the merits of all her children. The Church approaches with great respect and great compassion the experience of extermination, the *Shoah*, suffered by the Jewish people during World War II.[2]

A second consideration must be the context. The Vatican Council statement, *Nostra Aetate, Declaration on the Relationship of the Church to Non-Christian Religions*, October 28, 1965,[3] introduced a new era in the relationship of Jews and Catholics. More germane to our subject, however, was the establishment of the Commission for Religious Relations with the Jews [CRRJ] by Pope Paul VI on October 22, 1974. WR is the third of a series of related documents published by this Commission.

The first of these, issued on December 1, 1974, was entitled *Guidelines and Suggestions for Implementing the Conciliar Declaration Nostra Aetate (no. 4).*[4] The document itself expressed the conviction that nine years after *Nostra Aetate* was "...the right moment to propose...some concrete suggestions..." to implement it.[5] It refers only

once to the *Shoah*, and that briefly, but in dramatic terms links the
Vatican Council statement with the Holocaust:

> ...the step taken by the Council [*Nostra Aetate*] finds its historical set-
> ting in circumstances deeply affected by the memory of the persecution
> and massacre of Jews which took place in Europe just before and during
> the Second World War.[6]

Eleven years later, on June 24, 1985, the CRRJ promulgated the
*Notes on the Correct Way to Present the Jews and Judaism in
Preaching and Catechesis in the Roman Catholic Church.*[7] This
document dealt with topics such as "Relations between the Old and
New Testament," "Jewish Roots of Christianity," "The Jews in the
New Testament," "The Liturgy," and "Judaism and Christianity in
History." Pertinent to this paper is its reference to the *Shoah*, again
brief, but linking the *Shoah* to the preaching and religious teaching of
the Church: "Catechesis should...help in understanding the meaning
for the Jews of the extermination during the years 1939-1945, and its
consequences."[8]

A third and final consideration regarding WR is that it cannot be
interpreted as the Vatican's last word on the *Shoah*. The years of
preparation for the document, and the long anticipation generated by
this, could give the impression that this concludes the matter for the
Church. In fact, the contrary is true.

Dr. Eugene Fisher, Associate Director of the United States
Bishops Secretariat for Ecumenical and Interreligious Affairs, was in
Rome with a delegation of bishops and rabbis on the day that WR was
released. He describes Cardinal Cassidy as making it very clear that

> ...he does not see this as the close of discussion of the *Shoah*. Rather, it
> is a mandate for further dialogue and joint historical studies between our
> two communities. Those who see in it inadequacies are invited to join in
> the network of dialogical encounter to begin the process of a healing of
> memories, a reconciliation of histories. We Jews and Catholics need to
> bring together the best of our historical, sociological and theological
> thinking on the *Shoah*, not only for us but for all humanity.[9]

The International Catholic-Jewish Liaison Committee, in its communiqué at the conclusion of its meeting at the Vatican from March
23-26, 1998, reiterated this:

> Understanding the Vatican document on the *Shoah* as a beginning and
> not as an ending of a process, especially on the historical issues it raises,
> the Interfaith Liaison Committee as a whole expressed its commitment to
> continue the dialogue and to establish a joint working group of

historians and theologians to pursue further studies on the period of the *Shoah*, and to seek together a 'healing of memory.'[10]

Indeed, Cardinal Cassidy himself, in an address to the annual meeting of the American Jewish Committee in Washington on May 15, repeated his theme that WR is not "...the final word on the questions raised in the reflection."[11] The Cardinal also gave his opinion that he did not foresee any other Vatican statement on this subject in the near future. Others, however, differ with Cassidy in this regard.

Admittedly, then, WR does not conclude the process of interpreting and understanding the implications of the Holocaust for Catholics. As Cardinal Cassidy has suggested, however, it might be foolhardy to expect any kind of immediate follow-up or to anticipate, as some think, that the Pope himself will make some sort of grandiose and dramatic gesture of reconciliation during the jubilee year.

Nevertheless, the well-known American Jesuit theologian, Father Avery Dulles, is convinced that the Pope himself will issue "...his own pronouncement on the dark spots in Church history..." as he personally prepares for the millennium.[12] Likewise, the German theologian, Father Clemens Thoma, believes that "...the Pope should have no misgivings in submitting 'the Church as such' to the necessity of forgiveness," and this could occur through some sort of papal declaration during the jubilee year.[13]

Dulles' point of view has become more tenable as a result of a very recent statement of the Pope, the encyclical *Incarnationis Mysterium*. The Pope addresses this letter to "...all the faithful journeying toward the third millennium." John Paul II, in dramatic terms, speaks about the need of repentance during the jubilee year:

> As the successor of Peter, I ask that in this year of mercy the church...should kneel before God and implore forgiveness for the past and present sins of her sons and daughters.... Christians are invited to acknowledge before God and before those offended by their actions, the faults which they have committed.[14]

It is, at this point, of course, impossible to predict whether the Pope will, indeed, take any steps to offer acts of public repentance for past deeds by Church authorities, and, if he does so, whether the Holocaust would be included. What seemed highly unlikely, however, back in March 1998, now appears as far more possible.

It is accepted that WR is the third of a series of documents issued by the Commission for Religious Relations with the Jews, and uniquely among them, has the added prestige of a cover letter from Pope John Paul II. This is an understandable procedure typical of the practices of the offices of the Holy See. Nonetheless, one can wonder if this statement would have had greater impact if presented as a papal encyclical, or as a document issued and signed by the Pope himself (*motu proprio*). Proper bureaucratic procedures were followed, and this is not said critically, but what if the Pope had personally made these comments. It is possible to imagine that their effect might even have been greater than WR's. This is obviously conjecture, and, indeed, might have been far more difficult to achieve than WR. I believe, however, that the question remains pertinent, although, admittedly, not of primary importance given the already positive impression established by WR.

Reactions to *We Remember*

It would be of some benefit to survey the reaction of various commentators as they react positively or negatively to the various themes contained within WR. This has the additional advantage of pointing out those aspects of the document that have become contentious.

As one would expect, Catholic reaction has been generally, although not universally, favorable. Two colleagues of mine demonstrate this difference of opinion. Father Lawrence Frizzell, Director of the Institute of Judaeo-Christian Studies at Seton Hall University, lauded WR as a "...salutary challenge for those who strive to respond to the Pope's continuing work of spiritual and moral guidance which consistently has pointed to the Church's bond with the children of Israel."[15]

Another colleague, Sister M. Christine Athans, Professor of Church History at the St. Paul Seminary School of Divinity at the University of St. Thomas, described the document's goals as impressive, but its content as disappointing. As she wrote,

> ... (a) the historical overview is largely superficial and non-specific; (b) the references to Pope Pius XII fail to give an historical account of his role or to acknowledge the ongoing research and controversy concerning his unwillingness to condemn the Nazis during World War II.[16]

On the other hand, Father Dulles views the statement as written with "theological precision" and containing "notable strengths."[17]

Particularly pertinent and challenging to American Catholics was the joint statement issued by Cardinal William Keeler, Archbishop of Baltimore and Episcopal Moderator for Catholic-Jewish Relations, and Dr. Eugene Fisher. They welcomed the document and pointed out that its twin focus

...repentance for the past and hope for the future challenges Catholics in the United States in many ways. First, we must commit our resources, our historians, sociologists, theologians and other scholars, as the document mandates, to study together with their Jewish counterparts all the evidence with a view to a healing of memories, a reconciliation of history.

Second, we must look at the implications of this document for our educational programs, its opportunities for rethinking old categories as well as probing the most difficult areas of moral thought. To take the Holocaust seriously is to look at centuries of Christian misunderstandings both of Judaism and the New Testament itself, as the text emphasizes, and seek to replace them with more accurate appreciations of both. How shall we embody what this statement calls us to do in our classrooms and from our pulpits?[18]

Father John Pawlikowski, Professor of Social Ethics and the Catholic Theological Union in Chicago, considers WR as the most important document on Jewish-Catholic relations since *Nostra Aetate*. Nonetheless, he is concerned that it contains certain perspectives which he labels as "incomplete and sometimes even misleading."[19]

Jewish reaction to WR was far less complimentary. Rabbi Leon Klenicki, for example, Director of Interfaith Affairs for the Anti-Defamation League, and a person totally committed to Jewish-Christian understanding, wrestled with the question of why there was such "profound disappointment" among Jews over the publication of this long-anticipated document. He argues that with all the progress made in Jewish-Christian relations over the past three decades, and in the light of all the statements and actions of Pope John Paul II, a much stronger statement was expected. As he writes, "It was hoped that this document would culminate the process of reconciliation between Christianity and Judaism."[20] Nonetheless, the Rabbi admitted that "Disappointed as we are, we are nevertheless committed to continuing the creative interfaith dialogue that projects a message of hope to both faith communities."[21]

As was mentioned above, the International Catholic-Jewish Liaison met at the Vatican in late March 1998. This was a meeting scheduled many months before, but in the light of the publication of WR just a week before the members came to Rome, the delegates deviated from their original agenda to react to this new development. Dr. Gerhart Riegner, Honorary Vice-President of the World Jewish Congress and a co-chairman of the meeting, made two points in describing his reaction to WR. They are described in the conference communiqué in this way:

First, he as a personal witness to that tragic history,[22] stated that the Jewish community had been 'deeply impressed' by the 'very strong passages' in the document, citing in particular the acknowledgement of the need for 'repentance' (*teshuva*), on the part of the universal Church for the *Shoah*, the statement's 'binding commitment' to ensure that such evil does not happen again, and the willingness to review the painful history of past 'anti-Judaism' in the Church.

He nevertheless expressed serious disappointment that in his opinion the document 'avoids taking a clear position on the direct relationship between the teaching of contempt and the political and cultural climate that made the *Shoah* possible.' He furthermore expressed strong reservation concerning the document's presentation of some facts in the historical record.[23]

The participants in this meeting met with the Pope on March 26 at the conclusion of their discussions. On behalf of the Jewish participants, Geoffrey Wigoder of the Israel Interfaith Committee, addressed the Pope and repeated to him some of the criticisms raised by various Jewish leaders. Particularly difficult, Wigoder mentioned, was that the reflection of the Church was inadequate in linking the long history of religious anti-Semitism with the Catholic Church over the centuries to the indifference and even, at times, collaboration that was part of Catholic reaction to the *Shoah*. The Jewish leader complained that this aspect of Catholic-Jewish relations was not stated "unequivocally and with sufficient clarity."

Wigoder, however, concluded his remarks in a conciliatory and optimistic tone, affirming that "...Jews share the document's concluding hope that 'awareness of past sins' can be transformed into a firm resolve to build a new future on a shared mutual respect."[24]

Rabbi James Rudin, Director of the Interreligious Affairs Department of the American Jewish Committee, had a balanced reaction. He had hoped, as he said, for a stronger document from the Vatican, but believes that WR, "...Despite its ambiguities and ambivalence, represents not the end of the process but only the beginning."[25]

It would be beneficial also to take a brief look at Israeli reaction to WR. One publication has summarized Israeli Jewish leaders as being disappointed

...because the document falls short of placing responsibility on the Church itself for its silence during the *Shoah* and for the propagation of anti-Jewish teachings, through the centuries, that paved the way for the *Shoah*.[26]

The comments of two prominent Israelis, one a religious leader, the other, a scholar, demonstrate this attitude. The Chief Rabbi of Israel, Meir Lau, argued that WR did not satisfy the expectations that awaited the document. It was his opinion that one cannot rectify the errors of the past without reference to individuals involved. From this point of view, he concludes that "there is no doubt that a clear condemnation by the Vatican at that time would have had the force to stop the terrible things done during the *Shoah*."[27]

The well-known historian, Yehuda Bauer, focuses his reaction on the distinction made in the document between anti-Semitism and anti-Judaism. He writes:

> It may be true that Nazism was a neo-pagan ideology that attacked Christians as well, but the distinction drawn is anti-factual: Without Christian anti-Semitism there would have been no Nazi anti-Semitism.[28]

There is one other matter to discuss in this treatment of Jewish reaction to WR but it might be more appropriate to react to the above comments and realistically confront the dilemma caused by this document. Along with many others, I participated in conferences as far back as 1990 in Prague and 1992 in Baltimore, the purpose of which was to develop ideas of this projected Vatican document. I had long doubted, however, that any statement issued by the Vatican could ever please both Catholics and Jews. I felt that the frames of reference and the expectations were so divergent that criticisms, acrimony, and disappointment were bound to follow from one side or the other.

The situation was exacerbated by two additional factors. The preparation of this document was under consideration for over a decade and was, as indicated above, a subject for discussion at various Catholic-Jewish meetings. I note in passing that several years ago a preliminary version of the document was released without permission and caused quite a stir. Such a time period would certainly add to the conviction of those anticipating it and implicitly, if not explicitly, preparing to welcome a document that could be seen as the last word on the subject. Given the complexities of the history of the Holocaust, and the reaction of Pope Pius XII to it, such a view was naive at best and utopian at worst.

A second factor to be considered is the widespread positive impression caused by the statements of various episcopal conferences.[29] These different groups of bishops based their reflections on the real, concrete historical experience of the Holocaust as it transpired in their nations. They were able to speak specifically to their own people and to encourage a sense of repentance rooted in the common memories and sufferings that they all shared. It must be admitted that any statement issued by the Holy See would have to be directed to a far larger audience and such a specific approach would not have been possible. Realistic as this problem is, WR, nevertheless, caused disappointment to many because it did not contain the historical references, moral outrage and deep sense of contrition evident in some of the bishops' statements.

The World Jewish Congress' reaction to WR contains several aspects referred to here. The authors welcome its unequivocal approach to anti-Semitism, and see the document not only as an indictment of the past but also a milestone-guideline for the future."

Nevertheless, this prominent Jewish group, as many others, is most critical of the historical aspects of WR:

> Our problems with the Document relate to historical presentation and interpretation. However let us first say that the summary of the course of the *Shoah*, called 'a major fact of the history of the century,' should render impossible the obscenity of *Shoah* Denial among Catholics and we see in this one of the major positive aspects of the Document.

> Our disappointments in the historical treatment were accentuated by the great impression made upon us by the series of statements on the subject published in recent years by National Episcopal Conferences, especially in those countries which were the focus of the *Shoah*—many on the fiftieth anniversary of the liberation of the camps or the end of the European War. These documents were characterized by clarity, sensitivity and courage and we had hoped that the Vatican document would be written with the same categorical approach.[30]

To return to the subject of Jewish reaction to WR, ones sees a major, presumably unexpected, result. This is the renewed appeal by various Jews that the Holy See open its archives of the Holocaust period to scholars. It was, for example, a request made by the Jewish participants in the international Catholic-Jewish meeting held in Rome in late March and mentioned above. It is a theme frequently repeated in articles and editorials in various Jewish publications.

It should be no surprise that the United States Holocaust Memorial Museum is most anxious that all the Vatican records of the Holocaust period be made available. Its Council Chairman, Miles Lerman, had made this point very emphatically:

> I believe Jewish hearts and minds are open to the Pope's efforts to heal relations between the two faiths. It is, however, important to recognize that for such a process to take root, we must confront our past. The opening of the Vatican archives from this period would be the most effective means to accomplish the Pope's worthy goal.[31]

In an address on May 15, 1998, during a luncheon in honor of Cardinal Cassidy's first visit to the Holocaust Museum, Lerman made a similar, and, indeed, more pointed request:

> With few exceptions the Vatican's Holocaust-era archives have remained officially closed. The time has come for the Vatican to open its records and permit scholars to study the documents and reveal the pieces of history that are still missing.[32]

It should be noted, too, that Lerman, on this occasion, expressed the hope that the Museum would be the repository for these archives.

As someone who has worked extensively with the eleven volumes of diplomatic documents published by the Secretariat of State of the Holy See between 1965 and 1981, four volumes of which deal specifically with the "victims of the war," I fear sometimes that this contribution of the Vatican to historical research has not been clearly appreciated. Moreover, I suspect that the very existence of these primary sources has not been as well known as it should have been. Let all of us who are interested in studying and analyzing this period be grateful for this effort of the Holy See, and, as Cardinal Cassidy suggested in Rome, and repeated in similar terms in Washington,

> ...a joint team of Jewish and Catholic scholars [should] review the relevant material in the volumes produced by Catholic scholars covering the historical period concerned, and if questions still remain, they should seek further clarification.[33]

It has been the custom of the Holy See to release documents by pontificates. Available up to the present are the records to the end of the pontificate of Pope Benedict XV (1922). It would be expected that the successor of Pope John Paul II would allow access to the archives up to the end of the pontificate of Pope Pius XI (1922-1939).

Cardinal Cassidy's optimistic suggestion, however, has apparently had no effect on Vatican authorities. On December 3, 1998, the Holy See reaffirmed in very strong terms its long-standing contention that all pertinent materials concerning the Holocaust in the archives have already been published. The Director of the Vatican Press Office, Joaquin Navarro-Valls, indicated that the statement was a response to "accusations raised during the last several days against the Holy See." He was referring to a conference on the Holocaust sponsored by the State Department during which charges were made about the contents and availability of the Vatican archives.[34]

To conclude this section on WR, it would also be of interest to ascertain how the document was received by secular publications. The comments published in *Time* and the *New York Times* are pertinent to the subject of this paper. The former described WR's

> ...opening and closing segments...[as] irreproachable and historic. Calling the *Shoah* an 'unspeakable tragedy, which can never be forgotten,' the report styles itself an act of *teshuva*.... However, WR's middle

section is oddly parsimonious about the sins it admits. It includes and unexpectedly blunt denial that Christian anti-Judaism contributed to the Nazis' radical anti-Semitism....[35]

This *Time* article makes an additional point which is of interest to us in referring to the large non-European segment of the Roman Catholic Church who would have had little experience or knowledge of the Holocaust. It is the opinion of the *Time* writer that this audience could have influenced the authors of the document in their muted expression of possible guilt.[36]

A *New York Times* editorial considers WR a "...carefully crafted statement that goes further than the Roman Catholic Church has ever gone in reckoning honestly with its passivity during the Nazi era.... This breaking of new political and theological ground by the Vatican is important and welcome."[37]

The editorial also makes some points repeated elsewhere in this paper. It is very critical, however, of one aspect of the statement and refers to the oft-used inaccurate, but traditional, canard of the "silence of Pope Pius XII." In its analysis of WR's defense of Pius XII, the editorial found it "...regrettable that the Vatican has not yet found the courage to discard this defensive, incomplete depiction."[38]

It should be noted, too, that a different point of view was expressed in a *Newsweek* column, entitled "In Defense of Pius XII." The author describes some contemporary attitudes towards Pius XII as revisionism and writes:

> Something shameful is going on. That Pius XII was silent in the face of the Holocaust; that he did little to help the Jews; that he was in fact pro-German, if not pro-Nazi; that underneath it all he was anti-Semitic—all are monstrous calumnies that now seem to pass for accepted wisdom.[39]

Analysis: Positive and Negative Points

In continuing our discussion of WR, it must be kept in mind that the comments made in *Time* about the universal make-up of the Church are quite correct. The document is addressed to all Catholics, but for many hundreds of millions of them all that is known about Jews and Judaism is confined to the Bible. The Holocaust would not have the same significance for them as a shared and painful memory as it does for us.

WR has two focal points, two issues, that it attempts to address, the spiritual and the historical. Realistically it must be admitted that the methodology and goals of developing a sense of remembrance and repentance in the Christian context may differ from the methodology and goals used in historical analysis. It appears that the major disappointment of WR is that the passion and commitment to the spiritual objectives is not matched by a similar view in approaching the historical overview.[40]

The document makes it clear that Christians have been sinful, and quoting Pope John Paul II, that they have "departed from the spirit of Christ and His Gospel...and indulged in ways of thinking and acting which were truly forms of counter witness and scandal."[41]

I know, we all know, that in the sight of God this alienation from Christ and His teaching that has affected so many of those who call themselves Christian, has manifested itself in a myriad of ways over the centuries. WR, however, makes it startlingly clear that in this century the Nazi attempt to exterminate the Jews, the *Shoah*,[42] is the "unspeakable tragedy, which can never be forgotten." Christians cannot be "indifferent"[43] to this unprecedented tragedy, particularly because of the unique bonds between the Church and the Jewish people. Catholics are asked to meditate on this catastrophe, not just as some recollection of the past, but as a memory that lasts to a future outcome, that is "the moral imperative" that such hatred with its cataclysmic results should never happen again.

Preparation for the millennium is a key motif of WR, particularly in its first section. Catholics are encouraged to develop a millennial attitude based on remembrance and repentance. Singled out as an impetus to this attitude is the *Shoah*, the "worst suffering" of the Jews throughout their long history.

The second, very brief section, is entitled "What We Must Remember." There are three points to consider.

The faithfulness of the Jews to the "Holy One of Israel"[44] and to the Torah is described as a "unique witness." Indeed it is. In spite of repeated exiles, persecutions, massacres, discrimination of all sorts, false accusations and ghettoization, the Jews have remained faithful to their religion. What is so beautiful and touching about this recognition of Jewish witness in such a positive way is the realization of what a quantum leap it is from the traditional notion of the Jews as a "witness people."

For centuries, Jews in Christian lands, legally restricted in all kinds of ways, living on the periphery of Christian society, and reduced to second-class status, were labeled the "witness people." Their inferior status in Christian society, brought about, of course, by the ecclesiastical and political leaders of that society, was seen as part of God's will to punish them for their deicide. Christians were meant to rejoice in their own privilege and superiority as they observed the lowly position of the Jews. This was a theory with implications and applications that would affect the Jews over many centuries.[45]

I am also struck by the use of the word "inhumanity" as a description of Jewish suffering during the Holocaust. As the word "witness" did for those familiar with the history of Jews and Christians, so does this word resonate in the mind of any student of Holocaust history. I have long suggested to my students that the greatest crime of the Nazis may not simply have been the killing of so many Jews but the attempted indignity of dehumanization and depersonalization that preceded it. As the document states, this dehumanization "...is beyond the capacity of words to convey."

To attempt to deny and rob a person of his status as a child of God, uniquely created and gifted by Him, may be the greatest of crimes, and, particularly, when this was planned and orchestrated against the Jews by the Nazis.

The identification and control measures taken against the Jews led them to be herded into crowded ghettos and even more packed cattle cars. Starvation rations sometimes impelled them to fight each other for precious food. Medical and scientific experiments on certain Jews reduced them to the status of animals, and, in fact, on one occasion, Heinrich Himmler used the phrase "human animals" to refer to the Slavs, and *a fortiori*, to the Jews.[46]

The removal of children, the elderly and the sick from Jewish families was done in such a cruel fashion that it ignored all aspects of human love and family ties. This refusal to accept in Jews the same feelings that Germans had for their loved ones denied them their status as human beings. This dehumanization process might also have affected some Jews in the gas chambers of Auschwitz as they fought their fellow Jews to gain a minute or two more of life. Likewise, those Jews whose task it was to deceive their fellow Jews about the real purpose of the camp, to collect their belongings after they were gassed, and to throw their bodies into the furnaces or burning pits, must have reached a level of depersonalization.

The inhumanity of the Nazis toward the Jews must remain a haunting and sobering source of remembrance for all. We are blessed that the "witness" of the Jews to God and to the Torah, as well as their fidelity to *halachah*, has been documented and publicized. There were many Jews, who in spite of all Nazi efforts to depersonalize them, remained faithful to Judaism in whatever way they could, whether in the ghettos, labor camps, or death camps. This is rightly called spiritual resistance and was a blatant contradiction of all Nazi attempts to dehumanize them.

A third aspect of this section is the realistic admission that the *Shoah* took place in Europe, in countries with centuries of Christian tradition. This logically leads us to the relationship between the traditional anti-Jewish attitudes of Christians and the Holocaust. This, then, is the theme of the document's third section, "Relations between Jews and Christians," described at the outset as a "tormented" history, and one that "…has been quite negative."

In its sketchy treatment of Christian anti-Judaism which led to suspicion and mistrust of Jews by Christians, WR again uses a word that is an indictment of Christian treatment of Jews when it refers to the frequent "scapegoating" of the Jews. Jews were blamed for causing the Black Death of the fourteenth century and for becoming wealthy because of their money-lending practices and taking of Christian property. Everything evil or inexplicable was blamed upon the Jews. It would be a practice continued by Adolf Hitler as he blamed "Jewish traders" for the defeat of Germany in World War I and "international finance Jewry" for plunging the countries of Europe into a second war.

This earlier anti-Judaism would later be overshadowed by the rise of nationalism in the nineteenth century and by the development of racist theories which established a hierarchy of races.

It is true, as the document states, that both Popes Pius XI and Pius XII condemned racism, as it evolved under the Nazi government and similar regimes. These critiques, however, were equally directed against the growing "statism" of the German government and its attempt to practically deify itself. The words of outrage against racism by either Pope never specifically mentioned the Jews or anti-Semitism.[47]

Even though the protests of each Pope may not have had a great impact on us who read them six decades later, in the context of the times in which they were written, they certainly made an impression. I reread them for the purposes of this paper and believe that it would be beneficial to bring some aspects of each Pope's writings to your attention.

The best known of these protests is *Mit Brennender Sorge* ("With Burning Anxiety"), an encyclical addressed to the people of Germany by Pius XI in March 1937.[48] The Pope did not mention the Jews or anti-Semitism specifically in the encyclical but he made clear his condemnation of all forms of racism:

> Whoever exalts race, or the people or the State…whoever raises these nations above their standard value and divinizes them to an idolatrous level, distorts and perverts an order of the world planned and created by God….[49]

Pius continued by emphasizing that God's commandments are "…independent of time and space, of country and race." Again in strong words, the Pope wrote:

None but superficial minds could stumble into concepts of a national God, or of a national religion; or attempt to lock within the frontiers of a single people, within the narrow limits of a single race, God, the creator of the universe, King and Legislator of all nations....[50]

Moreover, in two places, the Pontiff scorned what he described as the "...so-called myth of race and blood," and the notion that revelation and faith could be used to justify such a concept.[51]

Pope Pius XII issued his first encyclical on October 20, 1939, some seven months after he was elected to the papacy and several weeks after the invasion of Poland and the start of the European war. The Latin title was *Summi Pontificatus*, which refers to Pius' "supreme pontificate" and, in the Roman style, is used as the title because it is the first two words of the statement. The subject matter of the encyclical is much more accurately indicated by its title in English, *The Unity of Human Society*.

The Pope points out two errors which he describes as destructive of peaceful relations between people. As he writes,

The first of these pernicious errors, widespread today, is the forgetfulness of that law of human solidarity and charity which is dictated and imposed by our common origin and by the equality of rational nature in all men, to whatever people they belong, and by the redeeming Sacrifice offered by Jesus Christ on the Altar of the Cross to His Heavenly Father on behalf of sinful mankind. [...]

And the nations, despite a difference of development due to diverse conditions of life and culture, are not destined to break the unity of the human race, but rather to enrich and embellish it by the sharing of their own peculiar gifts....[52]

In words that must be seen as particularly astute and realistic, the Pope deals with the second error:

But there is yet another error no less pernicious to the well-being of the nations and to the prosperity of that great human society which gathers together and embraces within its confines all races. It is the error contained in those ideas which do not hesitate to divorce civil authority from every kind of dependence upon the Supreme Being—First Source and absolute Master of man and of society—and from every restraint of a Higher Law derived from God as from its First Source. Thus they accord the civil authority an unrestricted field of action that is at the changeful tide of human will, or of the dictates of casual historical claims, and of the interests of a few.

Once the authority of God and the sway of His law are denied in this way, the civil authority as an inevitable result tends to attribute to itself that absolute autonomy which belongs exclusively to the Supreme Maker. It puts itself in the place of the Almighty and elevates the State or group into the last end of life, the supreme criterion of the moral and juridical order, and therefore forbids every appeal to the principles of natural reason and of the Christian conscience.[53]

I would have to conclude that this historical analysis of Jewish-Christian relations is so brief as to be inadequate. It is, of course, true, but ignores the question, indeed the dilemma, of the total absence of any statements from German bishops or the Vatican on racism once the war had started.[54]

It is the fourth section of WR, "Nazi anti-Semitism and the Shoah," that has generated the most criticism. There are a number of points to be considered and argued. WR distinguishes between the anti-Semitism of National Socialism and traditional anti-Judaism. This is a valid distinction. Anti-Judaism which can be traced back to the earliest days of the Christian Church has certainly been a major factor in the relations between Jews and Christians over the centuries. It is a prejudice or discrimination against the Jews because of their religion and their rejection of Christ and Christian teaching.

Unfortunately, this resulted at times in a treatment of the Jews that eerily foreshadowed (although not necessarily in a causative sense) the sufferings inflicted on the Jews by the Nazis. The yellow star or white armband, ghettoization, expulsion, expropriation of property and massacres, such an important part of the Holocaust, could all be viewed in retrospect in Jewish history in Christian lands.

The document describes this National Socialist ideology as refusing "...to accept any transcendent reality as the source of life and the criterion of moral good." Moreover, it was a denial of the "...constant teaching of the Church on the unity of the human race and on the equal dignity of all races and peoples...." There was "...a definite hatred directed at God Himself" in this attitude and little doubt that it would have eventually led to a campaign against Christianity itself, particularly Roman Catholicism with its international structure.

An interesting example of this distinction between anti-Judaism[55] and the National Socialist form of anti-Semitism may be seen in one constant response of the Holy See during the Holocaust. According to Catholic doctrine, those baptized Catholic are Catholic, and are to be recognized as such, independent of their ethnic or racial background. Whatever anti-Judaism may have existed up to that point ended at the time of baptism. In whatever country where anti-Semitic laws did not make an exception for baptized Jews, the nuncios and representatives of the Vatican would vigorously protest this infringement of the rights of the Church to determine its own membership. These repeated complaints, when baptized Jews continued to be defined as Jewish by various legal provisions and were not treated the same as other

Christians was certainly an effort by the Church to defend its own prerogatives, but it was also, at the same time, and this should be noted, a fundamental repudiation of Nazi racial theories.[56]

From this point of view, therefore, there is a distinction between the traditional anti-Judaism manifested by Christians over the centuries and the anti-Semitism of the Nazis. Nevertheless, it seems a bit simplistic for the document to state that "The *Shoah* was the work of a thoroughly modern neo-pagan regime...[whose] roots [were] outside of Christianity...." This, of course, is technically accurate but a bit ingenious in giving the impression that National Socialist ideology was without an etiology that was in any way Christian.

WR, however, to its credit, does confront this dilemma as it asks whether the anti-Jewish attitudes of so many Christians facilitated in some way the Nazi campaign against the Jews. The document asks a very powerful and, indeed, painful question:

> Did anti-Jewish sentiments among Christians make them less sensitive, or even indifferent,[57] to the persecution launched against the Jews by National Socialism when it reached power?

This is the ultimate question with which Christians of that time, as well as we ourselves today, must wrestle. It is, admittedly, a very nuanced and problematic issue to which there cannot simply be a definitive answer. WR speaks of the "multiple influences" that affected various people's attitudes and actions, and delineates them in this way:

> ...many people were altogether unaware of the 'final solution' that was being put into effect against a whole people; others were afraid for themselves and those near to them; some took advantage of the situation; and still others were moved by envy.

These four categories are obviously not meant to be exhaustive but do provide us with a range of personal reactions. It is mentioned later but I would wonder why at this point the document could not have referred to those Christians not affected by any of these influences, and whose witness to their Christian faith should be affirmed.

I fear, however, that WR begs the question by saying that the only response to the question must be sought on a case-by-case basis. Using this criterion, one could never suggest patterns of conduct or attitudes in any group.

We are asked to consider the two-step process that the Nazis used against the Jews, expulsion and, later, deportation. Expulsion was the earlier policy but it involved only the Jews of Germany, and after March 1938, Austria, as well. Equally true is the reluctance of any government to admit Jewish refugees.[58] I must admit, however, very frankly, that I resent the judgment that authorities in certain countries in North and South America (presumably the United States, chief among them), in refusing to admit Jews, have imposed upon them-selves "...a heavy burden of conscience." It may not be intentional but this can easily be interpreted as quite an offensive statement since an equivalent accusation is not made against authorities in countries some of whom collaborated when Jews were deported from their nations to labor camps, ghettos, and eventually to death camps.

Where is the *J'accuse* directed against the German authorities, the Catholic leaders of Slovakia and Croatia, the officials of Vichy France, all of whom were willingly involved in the deportation of Jews? Can the Vatican itself make judgments of other nations when its own representatives in London and Washington were instructed to do all possible to make known to the British and American governments its opposition to any notion of Palestine being a homeland or refuge for Jews fleeing Nazi persecution?[59] WR ignores the responsibility of all these authorities concentrating only on those of North and South America.

The document is justifiably and brutally honest in asking the pointed question: "Did Christians give every possible assistance to those being persecuted, and, in particular, to the persecuted Jews?" The reply to this question is, perhaps, the most controversial part of WR.

To the glory of Christianity, there were a number of Christians who aided the Jews in a variety of ways, even endangering their lives to do so. Several thousand of them are recognized and lauded by the State of Israel at Yad Vashem. The good deeds and sacrifices of many others are known only to God, although sometimes in personal conver-sations with survivors one hears remarkable stories of heroism and Christian concern for others.

I think here of an unknown Polish priest who cooperated in the subterfuge that took place in his village when a young Jewish girl who looked "Aryan" was taken in by a local Catholic family and raised as a niece of the family. In this situation she had to appear and act as Catholic in every way so as not to raise any suspicions about her origin. And so she did, with the knowledge and cooperation of this priest. She survived and has shared this poignant story with my students on many occasions. The heroism of this Polish family is memorialized at Yad Vashem. We do not know what happened to this parish priest who also risked his life on behalf of this young Jewish girl but I take the opportunity to salute him for his uniquely altruistic and Christian concern.

The acknowledgment of the life-saving activity of Pope Pius XII has led not only to dissension among historians but also to a sense of unease among Catholics loyal to the Church. WR proclaims:

> During and after the war, Jewish communities and Jewish leaders expressed their thanks for all that had been done for them, including what Pope Pius XII did personally or through his representatives *to save hundreds of thousands of Jewish lives.*[60]

Nevertheless, however, to read this praise of Pius XII without any reference to the controversy that surrounds his reaction to the Holocaust, appears almost surrealistic. One would not, and should not, expect a Vatican document to castigate or condemn Pius XII, and, indeed, it would be historically untenable to do so. The document loses some credibility in ignoring the criticism that has arisen from all sides by those attempting to interpret the Pope's actions during the Holocaust. This is not to insinuate that WR should have given voice to the various objections made against Pius XII, some of which, of course, border on hysteria, but it is an affirmation that the document should, at least, have admitted that the Pope's role during the Holocaust has been the subject of controversy.

We take note here of the comments made by Father Georges Cottier, the Pope's personal theologian, who reacted to some Jewish criticisms of WR, by stating that they concentrated too much on Pius XII and not enough on the document's call to repentance. As he said: "By shifting the attention to Pius XII, they end up losing sight of the central point of the text, which is its strong condemnation of the Holocaust."[61]

Father Cottier's comment is an appropriate reminder of the purpose of WR but, at the same time, it is difficult to ignore Pius XII who is mentioned twice in the text. That he remains a figure of controversy is a fact that cannot be denied. There is a growing tendency in our Church that appears almost revisionist to me in its thrust, to praise all the Pope's efforts and decisions during the Holocaust. Indeed, some see him as a very saintly person and his cause for canonization has been introduced. This, no doubt, is a reaction in part due to the unparalleled and unjustified vilification to which Pius XII has been subjected.

In a remarkable intervention, interpreted by many Catholics as intrusive and offensive, the Israeli Ambassador to the Holy See, Aharon Lopez, at the beginning of November 1998, asked for a fifty year moratorium on the procedure for the canonization of Pius XII. No matter what the Ambassador's motivation or rationale were, such a suggestion coming from someone outside the Church, will serve not only to buttress the position of those who see him as a much maligned Pope of great sanctity, but may, unfortunately, alienate other Catholics who would ordinarily be opposed or indifferent to his cause for canonization.[62]

Let us not deny either that revisionism also affects those who interpret the role of Pius XII in such a way as to give the impression that a single word or statement from him could have changed the whole outcome of the Holocaust. This school of thought would brand him as an anti-Semite who practically acquiesced in the killing of the Jews.

As with all extremes, the truth must be sought elsewhere. This is not the place for a detailed study of Pope Pius XII and the Vatican but it may be helpful to treat this topic briefly. The facts of Eugenio Pacelli's life and ecclesiastical career are well known, particularly his service as Nuncio to Bavaria and to Germany, and as Secretary of State to Pope Pius XI. What is frequently ignored, however, is any effort to understand, and the *sitz-im-leben* in which he conducted his papacy. The emotion attached to the interpretation of his role has blinded many to this and has led them to project back into his life aspects of contemporary society.[63]

I refer basically to Pius XII's ecclesiology, his view of the Church. It was an exclusivist approach. Protestants were heretics who denied certain tenets of Church teaching. Jews were outside the Church, their conversion was something to be prayed for since their covenant with God had been repudiated when they rejected and killed Christ, the Son of God. This was an expression of the anti-Judaism typical of the Pope's time, and prevalent among most Christians, whether Catholic or Protestant. It was quite antithetical to the racial anti-Semitism of the Nazis.

The corollary of this attitude is that the Jews would have had no place in the ecclesial vision of Pius XII. This is not the view of the Roman Catholic Church since Vatican Council II's declaration, *Nostra Aetate*, in 1965, which has led to an unprecedented appreciation of Jews and Judaism. Pope John Paul II has taught very clearly that the Jews are our elder brothers, that Judaism more than any other religion has a unique relationship to Christianity, and that God's choice of the Jews as His people, and His covenant with them, remains valid, vibrant and fruitful. As much as contemporary Catholic liturgy would amaze and shock Pius XII, so would such attitudes toward Judaism.

Jews and Judaism, therefore, had no great importance for Pope Pius XII. This is not to be interpreted as disdain for them, but as a realistic appreciation of their role in his world view.

This section, however, ends quite dramatically with a repetition of Pope John Paul's admission that "...the spiritual resistance and concrete action of...Christians was not that which might have been expected from Christ's followers." One could not have expected a more powerful statement or a more pained confession which puts upon Christians of today a "heavy burden of conscience."

WR entitled its fifth and last section "Looking Together to a Common Future." It would not be an exaggeration to say that this is a fitting conclusion to a document that has generated both positive and negative reactions. The authors of WR remind us that the Millennium requires Christians to express repentance for the sins and failures of those who have lived before them and that we approach "...with deep respect and great compassion the experience of extermination, the *Shoah*, suffered by the Jewish people during World War II."

It is ironic that, recently, Catholic commentators sympathetic to WR's call to repentance have come to suspect that it may be a goal far more difficult to achieve than originally imagined. According to this view, the Pope wanted the Church to look critically at its actions over the centuries, and ask forgiveness for those which contradicted Christian teaching and ideals. Two particular areas of concern were the treatment of the Jews over the centuries and the Inquisition. The Vatican sponsored symposia on each of these.

That WR is the result of the 1997 conference held in Vatican City,[64] and previous discussions held during the previous decade, is generally accepted. It may be simplistic but one could interpret WR's attempt to distinguish between the sins of members of the Church and the holiness of the Church itself as an effort to minimize some of the conference's conclusions.

Pertinent to this theme is the reaction to the conference on the Inquisition which has generated much negative feedback. One group, revisionists, do not want the Church to make any apology; another more moderate group questions how modern day Catholics can indicate sorrow for events and people whose historical context is totally alien to theirs.

One last aspect of this question is that Pope John Paul II himself, on two occasions, has wondered why other institutions, religions and leaders do not seem to be inclined to examine their failures over the past. In 1997, the Pope said: "What is interesting is that it is always the Catholic Church and the Pope who asks forgiveness. Meanwhile, others remain silent. But maybe that is the way it should be."[65]

I have criticized certain aspects of this document and praised others. As any human statement, WR is the result of earlier drafts, proposals, and compromises. With whatever faults or deficiencies it may have, it remains an impressive testament to the desire of the Catholic Church to repent for the failures of some of its members during the

Holocaust years. It expresses this in poignant terms as it looks back. In equally dramatic terms, it looks to the future:

> We pray that our sorrow for the tragedy which the Jewish people has suffered in our century will lead to a new relationship with the Jewish people. We wish to turn awareness of past sins into a firm resolve to build a new future in which there will be no more anti-Judaism among Christians or anti-Christian sentiment among Jews, but rather a shared mutual respect, as befits those who adore the one Creator and Lord and have a common father in faith, Abraham.

To this let us say AMEN!

NOTES

1. See Appendix A for the text of *We Remember*, as well as the Pope's letter. Individual citations of the document will not be listed in these endnotes.

2. Note the use of the Hebrew words, *teshuva* and *Shoah*. The latter is consistently used throughout the document.

3. See Appendix B for text of *Nostra Aetate*.

4. See Appendix C for the text of the *Guidelines*.

5. *Ibid.*, p. 2.

6. *Ibid.*

7. See Appendix D for text of the *Notes*.

8. *Ibid.*, p. 9.

9. Statement released by Dr. Fisher on May 20, 1998; originally published in *The Jerusalem Report*, April 16, 1998, p. 38.

10. *Origins*, April 9, 1998, p. 704.

11. *Ibid.*, May 28, 1998, p. 30; see also *Perspectives on We Remember: A Reflection on the Shoah* (New York: American Jewish Committee, 1998), p. 6.

12. *America*, April 4, 1998, p. 3.

13. Hans Hermann Henrix, *The Vatican Text, We Remember: A Historical Document?* p. 4; unpublished.

14. *Incarnationis Mysterium*, November 29, 1998; see *Origins*, December 10, 1998, p. 450.

15. *An Initial Response by a Catholic Thinker*; unpublished.

16. *Do Not Fear to Tell the Truth*; unpublished.

17. *America*, April 4, 1998, p. 4.

18. *Origins*, March 26, 1998, p. 675. It is truly a matter of hope and optimism that the Secretariat for Ecumenical and Interreligious Affairs of the National Conference of Catholic Bishops, of which Dr. Fisher is the Director, has arranged a Holocaust Education Conference to be held in Baltimore in mid-February 1999. It is co-sponsored by the Archdiocese of Baltimore and the American Jewish Committee. Specifically germane to our subject is that Cardinal Cassidy will address the topic, *We Remember: A Reflection on the Shoah—One Year Later*.

19. Essay on *We Remember*, p. 2; unpublished.

20. *New Jersey Jewish News*, March 19, 1998, p. 6.

21. *Ibid.*

22. Dr. Riegner was the representative of the World Jewish Congress in Geneva during the Holocaust years.

23. Communique of the International Catholic-Jewish Liaison Committee Meeting, Vatican City, March 23-26, 1998; *Origins*, April 9, 1998, p. 703.

24. *Ibid.*

25. *Perspectives*, p. 24.

26. *Christians and Israel: A Quarterly Publication from Jerusalem*, Spring 1998, p. 3.

27. *Ibid.*

28. *Ibid.*

29. A new publication (September 1998) contains these statements by the Hungarian (1994), German (1995), Polish (1995), American (1995 and 1997), Dutch (1995), Swiss (1997), French (1997) and Italian (1998) bishops. See Secretariat for Ecumenical and Interreligious Affairs, National Conference of Catholic Bishops, *Catholics Remember the Holocaust* (Washington, DC: United States Catholic Conference, 1998).

30. World Jewish Congress. International Jewish Committee on Interreligious Consultation, *Response to Vatican Document "We Remember: A Reflection on the Shoah,"* p. 1.

31. *Washington Post*, July 1, 1998, p. A23.

32. *The Vatican Remembers: But the World Must Know* was the title of the address given at the luncheon.

33. *Origins*, April 9, 1998, p. 703.

34. Navarro-Valls categorically denied that anything about the Holocaust could be found in the Vatican archives and added that "Anyone who makes insinuations contrary to what the Holy See has already repeated several times should have some concrete evidence—which, naturally, will not be forthcoming." *The Catholic World Report*, January 1999, pp. 7-8; see also *America*, December 19, 1998, p. 4.

35. *Time*, March 30, 1998, p. 60.

36. *Ibid.*

37. "The Vatican's Holocaust Report," *New York Times*, March 18, 1998, p. A20.

38. *Ibid.*

39. Kenneth L. Woodward, *Newsweek*, March 30, 1998, p. 35.

40. I find it very interesting and appropriate the seven areas of strength in WR detailed by Philip Cunningham in a Panel Discussion on May 6, 1998, and published in *The Catholic Church and the Holocaust: Perspectives on the Vatican Statement We Remember: A Reflection on the Shoah* (Hartford, Trinity College: Center for Study of Religion in Public Life), pp. 6-8.

41. See Appendix A, individual citations will not be given for WR.

42. It is noteworthy that throughout the document the Hebrew term *Shoah* is consistently used for Holocaust. This, of course, is another indication, if one were needed, that revisionism is not an approach acceptable to the Holy See.

43. I see in the use of this word "indifference" a possible reference to the words of Pope John Paul II when he visited Auschwitz on June 7, 1979. He said: "This inscription [Hebrew] awakens the memory of the people whose sons and daughters were intended for total extermination.... It is not permissible for anyone to pass by this inscription with *indifference*." See Pope John Paul II, *Spiritual Pilgrimage: Texts on Jews and Judaism, 1979-1995*, Eugene J. Fisher and Leon Klenicki, eds. (New York: Crossroad, 1995), p. 7.

44. Note the use of this term which would be the traditional Jewish practice instead of using the name of God.

45. See Edward H. Flannery, *The Anguish of the Jews: Twenty-Three Centuries of Antisemitism* (New York: Paulist Press, 1985).

46. See Lucy Dawidowicz, ed., *A Holocaust Reader* (New York: Behrman House, 1976), p. 131.

47. The so-called "hidden encyclical" of Pope Pius XI, *Humani Generis Unitas*, dealt specifically with anti-Semitism while at the same time repeating traditional supersessionist arguments against the Jews. See Georges Passelecq and Bernard Suchecky, *The Hidden Encyclical of Pius XI*. Translated by Steven Rendall (New York: Harcourt Brace & Company, 1997).

48. The English translation of *Mit Brennender Sorge* may be found in *The Catholic Mind*, May 8, 1937, XXXV:9, pp. 185-204; see a more detailed study of this topic in John F. Morley's *Pope Pius XI and the Holocaust*, a paper given at the First Biennial Conference on Christianity and the Holocaust, Rider University, April 22, 1990, and published in the Conference Proceedings.

49. *Ibid.*, p. 188.

50. *Ibid.*, pp. 189-190.

51. *Ibid.*, pp. 191, 195.

52. Claudia Carlen, IHM, ed., *The Papal Encyclicals 1939-1958* (Raleigh: McGrath Publishing Company, 1981), pp. 10, 11.

53. *Ibid.*, p. 12.

54. Admittedly, *Summi Pontificatus* was published a few months after the war had begun.

55. See John F. Morley, *Anti-Judaism in the Christian Context – Modern Times*, paper given at the symposium on *The Roots of Anti-Judaism in the Christian Context*, Vatican City, October 30-November 1, 1997.

56. See John F. Morley, *Vatican Diplomacy and the Jews during the Holocaust, 1939-1943* (New York: KTAV, 1980).

57. See the comments on the use of this word in note 40.

58. The Evian Conference of July 1938 demonstrated how shallow was the resolution of the nations participating to actually help and accept into their countries Jewish refugees from Germany.

59. Morley, *Vatican Diplomacy, passim.*

60. Emphasis mine; the source for this large number is more than likely Pinchas E. Lapide, *Three Popes and the Jews* (New York: Hawthorne Books, 1967). He writes on pp. 214-15:

> To which we may add, in the light of the preceding chapters, that the Catholic Church, under the pontificate of Pius XII was instrumental in saving at least 700,000, but probably as many as 860,000 Jews from certain deaths at Nazi hands.... The final number of Jewish lives in whose rescue the Catholic Church had been instrumental is thus at least 700,000 souls, but in all probability is much closer to the maximum of 860,000. It was as if this crusade of rescue was meant to atone, in part, for the hateful teachings of the past. These figures, small as they are in comparison with our six million martyrs whose fate is beyond consolation, exceed by far those saved by other churches, religious institutions and rescue organizations combined.

61. *Origins*, March 26, 1998, p. 675.

62. *Inside the Vatican*, December 1998, pp. 17-19. It should be noted, however, that the Ambassador's comments may have been a diplomatic tit-for-tat in response to Archbishop Jean-Louis Tauran's statement, made in Jerusalem itself, that "East Jerusalem is illegally occupied." The Archbishop is a high-ranking Vatican diplomat, whose remarks must be seen as reflecting Vatican thinking.

63. See Father John Pawlikowski's interpretation of Pius XII's activities in "Pius XII and the Jews: Further Research, Please," *Commonweal*, July 17, 1998, pp. 8-9.

64. I participated in this Conference on Anti-Judaism held in Vatican City itself between October 30 and November 1, 1997, presenting a paper entitled *Anti-Judaism in the Christian Context – Modern Times*.

65. For this information, I am indebted to a column entitled "Examining the Church's Conscience Isn't Easy," by John Thavis in *The Catholic Advocate*, January 6, 1999, p. 13.

4

Reaction of a Protestant Theologian to the Vatican's *We Remember* Document

Franklin H. Littell

On March 12, 1998 the Vatican, headquarters of the Roman Catholic Church, issued from Rome a powerful statement on the *Shoah*. Entitled "We Remember: A Reflection on the *Shoah*," the message to the faithful was communicated through the Vatican Commission for Religious Relations with the Jews. This Commission is chaired by one of the key prelates of the Church, an Australian who is also the Church's point man in relation to other religions: Cardinal Edward Idris Cassidy.

The importance of the message is signified by its doctrinal content, to which we shall return. But also—and this is a vital point that outsiders can easily miss—the importance of the message in the mind of the Church's leadership is indicated by its place on the agenda of the Church and in the Church's calendar.

In the Church's changing interpretation of the meaning of the Jewish people's role in history, the lessons of centuries of denigration have been relegated to the trash can. Not long ago, and without embarrassment before the Holocaust, the Roman Catholic Church and other churches still preached and taught that Jewish survival was an unfathomable mystery. The lesson was clear: the Christian church had superseded the Jewish people in the providence of God, the "New Israel" had inherited the promises from the "old Israel," the time of the Messiah had been entered upon by a remnant of the formerly Chosen—joined to the Elect of the gentiles. In the self-definition of the churches, a wandering and suffering Jewish people was now at best only a marginal note to the pages of a triumphant Christian history.

From John XXIII to John Paul II

In "We Remember" this teaching of contempt has been rejected dramatically, with deep regret expressed for its past consequences. John Paul II, whose long years as Pope have been singularly fruitful in effecting the rethinking and reworking of Catholics' perception of and relations with the Jewish people, has now fixed the issue in the calendar of *preparation for the third millennium* of Christian history. The

71

season of approach to the year 2000 Anno Domini is to be, spiritually, shaped by the forgiveness of sins and reconciliation. Christians in Asia and Africa (which within two more generations will have the majority of the Christians of the world) might easily be tempted to pass off the guilt for the Holocaust to Europe or even Germany alone, but they are called back by a papal message *addressed to the World Church*. Along with the blessings of the faith, they must share the shame for the misdeeds of fellow-Christians. Most of all, the doctrinal form of the Message will be the same in all parts of the *Ecumene*: no sector is exempted from the burden of remembering the *Shoah*.

More than that, the Pope speaks in "We Remember" to "Catholics and Jews and *all men and women of good will*," using a phrase that outsiders welcomed in Pope John XXIII's language in "Pacem in Terris" (April 10, 1963). John Paul II also ties his concern for Christian/ Jewish reconciliation to the more general issue of human rights, to the goal of achieving "true respect for the life and dignity of every human being." Here again we find a connection with the spirit and achievements of his great predecessor, whose encyclicals "Mater et Magistra" (May 15, 1961) and "Pacem in Terris" had set direction signs for Christian position papers on human rights.

Pope John XXIII, whose diplomatic posts during World War II had brought him into direct and compassionate contact with Jews under the Nazi assault, had initiated the first major effort to transform the Roman Catholic Church's understanding of the right Christian relationship to the Jews. Because of heavy opposition from conservative churchmen, and especially too because of the intense diplomatic pressure of several Arab governments, it proved impossible for the Vatican at that time to make a clean break from the centuries of theological and cultural anti-Semitism in European "Christendom." Confronted by religious and cultural anti-Semitism, both internal and external,[1] the Church Fathers were unable politically to address directly the issue of correcting Christian teaching about the Jews. Wrong and negative words and phrases could be removed, but settling upon a form of words to affirm Jewish survival and well-being was far more difficult.

In Vatican II, the theme of Christian-Jewish relations was tossed back and forth between the group working on ecumenical relations and the group defining the attitude to other religions. Many wished to distinguish inter-church from interreligious relations. Others argued that neither historically nor doctrinally could the Christian relationship with Judaism and Jewry be equated with the contact with other world religions. To avoid losing the entire theme from the Council findings, a section on "the spiritual bond linking the people of the New Covenant with Abraham's stock" was written into the "Declaration on the Relationship of the Church to Non-Christian Religions" (*Nostra Aetate*).[2] It appears directly following the section on the relationship with those of "the Islamic faith." Pope Paul, who had succeeded upon John XXIII's death, released the Declaration on October 28, 1965.

The uneasy relationship of Christians and Jews was being redefined in the churches. But apart from governmental circles directly concerned with survivors, the explosive topic of the Holocaust still came up only in unofficial circles of academics and churchmen. The Protestant commentator on *Nostra Aetate* in the volume of documents edited by Walter Abbott, S.J. pointed out that the World Council of Churches meeting in New Delhi in 1961 also found it impossible at that time to utter a word on the issue that was quietly becoming the most lively topic in informal discussions and tracts for the times: Christian guilt for the centuries of persecution of the Jews, culminating in the Holocaust.

At New Delhi, as at Vatican II, resistance to change came from defenders of traditional theological anti-Semitic positions, especially from delegates of Christian churches precariously situated in areas controlled by Muslim regimes. The church judicatories, whether European or American, Roman Catholic or Protestant, were not yet ready to face the implications of the Holocaust for "Christendom" and its preaching and teaching.

Vatican II (1961-65) could not yet bring the Church to positive affirmations about the Jewish people, but the process of purging the liturgies and the catechetical materials of negative notes was begun. A major doctrinal victory was won in *Nostra Aetate*, however: the "deicide calumny," the charge that the whole Jewish people were originally and remain indefinitely guilty of the crucifixion, was rejected.

Nostra Aetate had run up against immediate resistance, both doctrinal and political. At that time, throughout much of the world church it was thought—like the "Declaration on Religious Freedom" (*Dignitatis Humanae*)—to reflect a peculiarly American history and set of mind toward toleration and liberty. Thirty-five years later, however, there was a readiness throughout much of the Church for a further march forward, and in it a solid push was coming from German theologians and agencies.

The transition from resistance to acceptance to anticipation of further progress has been marked by significant changes in the teachings and their concrete application. During the 1960s there were carried through painstaking and comprehensive scholarly investigations of the Roman Catholic Church's high school textbooks and catechetical literature,[3] to identify and delete references at odds with the Church's new direction. The *Guidelines for Ecumenical and Interreligious Affairs* of 1975, followed by the 1985 *Notes*, illuminated the line of march. The *Guidelines* stressed that the Church's own self-definition is welded to "the mystery of Israel." Progress was slow but steady, and much of it took place behind the curtains.

European Churches and Holocaust Education

We might at this point take a side glance at the developments in the German Protestant establishments, where the religious dimension of the Holocaust was faced earlier and in more depth than elsewhere in the Protestant world. At the Berlin *Kirchentag* of 1961 *Arbeitsgruppe VI*—"on Jewish and Christian relations"—was launched and it became a regular and packed section of the large laymen's gathering. Each year thousands attended, listening to panels of Jewish and Christian leaders and sending forward on slips of paper small mountains of questions. In the following decade the unmentionable topic—the genocide of the Jews—worked its way to the surface of the meeting and into the consciousness of the parishes. On June 6-9, 1975 the first German Consultation on the Holocaust was held at Haus Rissen, Hamburg, sponsored jointly by the National Conference of Christians and Jews and the German Councils of Christians and Jews.

In January of 1980, after five years of intensive study in the parishes of the Protestant Church of the Rheinland, the Synod adopted the most self-critical and thorough-going post-Auschwitz appraisal of Christian preaching and teaching to appear from any church judicatory to this day (1999). It would be diversionary to discuss the Rheinland judicatory action at length, but its existence documents the way in which the interaction of Jews and Protestants and Roman Catholics has shaped the thinking of all three faiths.

Note these phrases picked from a long set of basic affirmations of Jewish survival and well-being:[4]

> The continuing existence of the Jewish people, its return to the Land of Promise, and also the creation of the State of Israel, are signs of the faithfulness of God toward God's people.

> Stricken, we confess the co-responsibility and guilt of German Christendom for the Holocaust.

> We believe in the permanent election of the Jewish people as the people of God....

> We believe that in their calling Jews and Christians are always witnesses of God in the presence of the world and before each other. Therefore we

are convinced that the church may not express its witness toward the Jewish people as it does its mission to the peoples of the world.

In the initial stage, the German Protestant rethinking reflected the influence of the Church Struggle (*Kirchenkampf*), both in the personal histories of its second-generation leaders (Eberhard Bethge, Heinz Kremers, Franz von Hammerstein, Martin Stöhr *et alia*) and in affirmation of "the new biblical insights concerning the continuing significance of the Jewish people for salvation history (e.g., Rom. 9-11), which have been attained in connection with the Church Struggle."[5]

As the discussion has matured, the leading German Protestants have—like the most significant German Catholics—situated the Holocaust as the turning point in their thinking about the relations of Christians and a not only surviving, but flourishing world Jewry. The students of the theology professors show up as volunteers on the *kibbutzim*, as student-workers in the *Aktionsühnezeichen* center in Jerusalem, and in the seminars on the Holocaust at Hebrew University.

For a specific German example of the post-Auschwitz scholar and activist, take Professor Martin Stöhr. As Director of the Church Conference Center *Arnoldshain*, he made it a major year-round base of Christian-Jewish dialogue, with a continuous stream of conferences and publications. He founded the major program sending German students to Israel: *Studium am Israel*. During a subsequent decade as Theology Professor at Siegen he remained an activist as well as scholar, leading the German Association of Councils of Christians and Jews and thereafter serving as President of the International Council of Christians and Jews during its great expansion into the countries of eastern Europe that followed the collapse of the Soviet empire in 1989.

The name of Catholic theologian Hans Küng of Tübingen is also well known across the world map of persons active in Christian-Jewish dialogue. Another key Roman Catholic has been Dr. Ansgar Koschel, Executive Director of the *Koordinierungsrat der Gesellschaften für christlich-jüdische Zusammenarbeit*. In the start-up of international interreligious work after World War II, and especially in support of seminars and conferences on the Holocaust, the National Conference of Christians and Jews (USA) was the heavy-weight. Today the united German Councils are the strongest force in the International Council of Christians and Jews, which today includes more than twenty national units.

The spirit of transformation has been working also in ecclesiastical circles. The "Declaration of Repentance" delivered at the site of the Drancy transit camp by the French bishops, on September 30, 1997, precisely during the trial of former Vichy official Maurice Papon, sounds a direct note of repentance for the failure of the Church vis-à-vis French Jewry: "Today we confess that silence was a mistake. We also acknowledge that the Church of France at that time failed in its mission of educating consciences and that she thus bears with the Christian people the responsibility of not having helped rescue in the early stages when protest and protection were possible and necessary...." The statement concludes in a personal, involved mood: "We acknowledge this reality today because this failure of the Church of France and its responsibility toward the Jewish people are part of its history. We confess this sin. We beg God's forgiveness and ask the Jewish people to hear our words of repentance."[6]

The Declaration of the German Catholic bishops on the Shoah has also gone deep, and it joined the French bishops' statement in creating a situation where those concerned throughout the Church were already talking of the next steps to be taken—perhaps especially in the Church observances of the year 2000 A.D. Where *Nostra Aetate* was met with determined resistance from many quarters of the Church, many sectors today are criticizing "We Remember" for being too mild.

Progress on the American Scene

Official interreligious cooperation, on the Holocaust as well as other matters, was slow to come. Roman Catholics were not officially permitted to participate until Vatican II. But there were non-theological factors at work. It is surely symbolic that the very first joint statement ever issued by the Protestants (Federal Council of Churches) and the Roman Catholics (US Catholic Bishops) was a solid protest over the 1938 *Kristallnacht* pogrom in Germany.

Public acceptance of interreligious dialogue in America was well out in front of the denominational officials. Its acceptability to laymen was greatly influenced by the experience of servicemen during World War II. "Cooperation Without Compromise" actually worked in the mutual aid developed by rabbis, priests and ministers in the chaplaincy. Another important public impetus came through the National Conference of Christians and Jews (NCCJ). In 1950 there returned to the States, to assume top positions in the NCCJ, several persons who had held key positions in the Education and Religious Affairs division of the Office of Military Government (US). Two of those most senior were Roman Catholics (James Egan, Dumont Kenney) and one was a Protestant (C. Arild Olsen, who later became Associate Director of the National Council of Churches). In the American occupation of Germany they had worked with German churchmen and professors to foster ecumenical and interreligious cooperation in the preparation of school texts, the founding of church conference centers (*evangelische*

Akademien and *katholische Sozialakademien*), the holding of dozens of seminars and conferences, the promotion of interreligious dialogue, the furtherance of democratic principles in labor unions and professional associations, etc.

For two decades, the NCCJ was a major force in developing inter-religious projects in cities across the country and—through the Association for the Coordination of Religious Affairs (f. 1959)—on dozens of campuses. During the first decade of its existence, the Annual Scholars' Conference on the Holocaust and the Churches was also greatly helped by NCCJ money and personnel.

Thus, while the major part of the American churches were slowly working their way toward a major change from the teaching of contempt, the public was being prepared by veterans of World War II and former officers in the subsequent American Military Government to accept the idea that citizens of a democracy worked together in the national interest regardless of faith differences.[7]

There were other signs of the way events in the Jewish community were influencing Christian awareness of the issue of Jewish death and survival. In 1961 Elie Wiesel's *Night* and the first edition of Raul Hilberg's *The Destruction of the European Jews* began to awaken English-language general readers to the significance of the Nazi assault on the Jewish people.

In 1962 the Eichmann Trial impacted the Israeli school lessons and the educational program for the young soldiers in the Israel Defense Forces (IDF). This was the turning point in Israeli awareness of the Holocaust, and that awareness seeped outward into the diaspora. From the dramatic opening address by the freshly appointed Attorney General, Gideon Hausner—"I speak for the six million!"—to Eichmann's death sentence for genocide, the trial was an educational experience for the citizens of Israel.[8] Its significance also slowly penetrated the awareness of American Jews and their immediate friends.

On the large map, it was the threat to Israel's existence in 1967, when a combined attack by Arab League powers threatened a "second Holocaust," that activated American Jewry and a considerable body of American Christians to organize and take action for Jewish survival.[9] Three new agencies dealing with the key facets of Christian-Jewish understanding—Holocaust, Israel, a revised Christian theology of the Jewish people—were founded at that time, and still flourish.

The change within American Catholicism was also quiet, beyond public scrutiny. In 1945 the official position remained that Roman Catholics might only cooperate openly with Jews and Protestants—as fellow-citizens—on two fronts: one, in organizing anti-Communist action; two, on common civic concerns, such as police and public

safety, schools, the upkeep of public parks, etc.[10] Interreligious cooperation with visible Roman Catholic participation was carried on quietly
in a few places—University of Iowa, University of Michigan, Cornell
University. The breakthrough to open interreligious dialogue which
included the Roman Catholics came with Vatican II (1961-65).

What progress was made in the following decade was attained
chiefly in unofficial and voluntary associations. Officially, in American
Protestant circles little seemed to change during the 1960s and 1970s.
Gerald Strober, a Presbyterian scholar, made a study in 1972 for the
National Conference of Christians and Jews and the American Jewish
Committee, to determine what changes had occurred since Bernhard
Olson made his famous study[11] and analysis of hostility to Jews and
Roman Catholics in Protestant teaching materials.

Olson's study paralleled major analyses of Roman Catholic and
Jewish lesson materials and the attitude to the other two, carried out at
St. Louis University and Dropsie College, Philadelphia. He studied the
church school curricula of four representative schools of thought—neo-
orthodox, traditional conservative, liberal and fundamentalist. He found
a "marked prominence" of "the Jew" in all four, but a greater anxiety
at the rise to power and prominence of Roman Catholicism. Strober
confined his 9-year study[12]—*Portrait of the Elder Brother: Jews and
Judaism in Protestant Teaching Materials*—to twelve Protestant
denominations and about 3,000 lessons. He found the traditional
Christian theological anti-Semitism to be the rule still, with Jesus and
the disciples portrayed in such a way as to "convey the impression that
they were somewhat not Jews;" Judaism itself, when mentioned, was
portrayed as a fossil; attributing "blood guilt" and "collective guilt" for
the crucifixion was still general. Most striking of all, of approximately
3,000 lessons only six mentioned the Holocaust; only four specifically
dealt with the Jewish sector in the death camps, and *only one* of those
with sensitivity and in depth. Only 15 lessons, less than half of one per
cent, mentioned the State of Israel—and nine of these were dispensa-
tionalist. Strober concluded, "There is no evidence so far that these
painful yet essential issues are being confronted in Protestant teaching."[13]

At the end of the two decades, a veritable explosion of college
courses, seminars and conferences, published articles and books
revealed the ferment that had been going on below the surface. The
attention of the American public—Jews and Christians and others of
conscience—was gathered up by the drive for a US Holocaust
Memorial Museum (opened in 1993) and the official observance of
Yom Hashoah from 1980 on. In America interreligious cooperation at
the level of good citizenship has reached, perhaps, its symbolic high

point in the Jewish and Protestant and Roman Catholic effort which produced the US Holocaust Memorial Museum and the marking of Yom Hashoah[14] as an official day on the American calendar. By early 1999, over 15,000,000 visitors have come to the Museum, and the Holocaust Day of Remembrance is officially observed with declarations and services at the Congress and most legislatures. Every governor and the mayor of every major city issues a proclamation annually.

Methodists and Mennonites and the Genocide of the Jews

In the meantime the theological issues raised by the Holocaust remain fluid. There were many denominational statements indicating ferment after 1970, with change even more evident after 1980. The Lutheran (ELCA) statement of 1985 is often cited.

For comparison with the development among American Catholics we may look briefly at two well-known American Protestant churches, one large and the other small.

The Methodists

In its General Conference of 1972 the United Methodist Church urged its members to engage in dialogue with Jews. Following the General Conference of April, 1996, a statement was issued that introduced the imperative call to dialogue with the observation that "especially crucial for Christians in our quest for understanding has been the struggle to recognize the horror of the Holocaust as the catastrophic culmination of a long history of anti-Jewish attitudes and actions in which Christians, and sometimes the Church itself, have been deeply implicated."

In this recent Methodist statement both Jewish and Christian covenants with God are termed "eternally valid" and the belief is expressed that God "has continued, and continues today, to work through Judaism and the Jewish people." In a direct and personal way, the statement calls for repentance: "As followers of Jesus Christ we deeply repent of the complicity of the Church and the participation of many Christians in the long history of persecution of the Jewish people. [...] In the twentieth century there is particular shame in the failure of most of the Church to challenge the policies of governments that were responsible for the unspeakable atrocities of the Holocaust."[15]

Similar statements, reflecting the Protestant capacity for sharp criticism of the institutional church itself, have been released during the last decade by other major churches based in the United States.

The Mennonites

In a strong 1985 statement from a small but historic Protestant church body—the Mennonites—we find several notes not common to those of the larger and more assimilated denominations.[16] In "Mennonite Witness as it Relates to Jewish People," in the midst of some statements of traditional Christian views, we find striking flashes of new insight. "In acknowledging that Christendom in its faithlessness to its Lord has too often represented a threat, lostness and death to Judaism, we recognize the need for the organized church, of which we are a part, to engage in self-examination." The special connection between the Jewish people and the Land is recognized: "Israel re-gathered is evidence that God has not forgotten the people He has known from ancient times in covenant relationship. [...] We affirm a positive stance toward the state of Israel...."

True to the Anabaptist tradition, the Mennonite statement links the alienation between Christians and Jews to the rise of "Hellenized and Romanized Gentile Christianity" in the era after the Christian Emperor Constantine the Great. The reference to this point in church history, sometimes called "the fall of Christianity" by Protestant radicals, is made even more pointed by the Mennonites' acknowledgement

> that during the heyday of triumphalistic Christendom, the Jewish people in "Christian" lands far more faithfully reflected the character of Jesus than did the Gentile church of the West.[17]

The perspective of the Mennonites reminds us vividly of the judgment of Jules Isaac, a French Jew and scholar: "I say and maintain that the fate of Israel [i.e., the Jewish people] did not take on a truly inhuman character until the fourth century A.D. with the coming of the Christian Empire."[18]

Parallel Developments in the World Council of Churches

There are remarkable parallels between the developing thought of the ecumenical movement and the development in Roman Catholicism from *Nostra Aetate* to "We Remember."

At the First General Assembly of the World Council of Churches (WCC) in 1948, "the special meaning of the Jewish people for Christian faith" was acknowledged. Anti-Semitism was denounced as "a sin against God and man." The Third Assembly (New Delhi, 1961) rejected the notion that Jews today share in guilt for the death of Christ. (At the same time Vatican II was also expunging the deicide calumny.) In a document commended to the churches for study and action in 1982, the Executive Committee of the WCC critically noted specific negative roles and images in the traditional Christian references to the Jews' role in salvation-history:

- The abrogation of the Sinai covenant;

- The replacement of Israel as God's people by the Church;

- The destruction of the Temple as proof of divine rejection of the Jewish people; and

- Ongoing Judaism as a fossilized religion of legalism.[19]

The WCC's Consultation on the Church and the Jewish People, meeting at Sigtuna, Sweden in 1988, reached another level in the dialogue: the right of self-definition by the sundry parties to the dialogue was affirmed.[20] This contradicted squarely the venerable Christian custom of "dictating the role of the Jews in another religion's drama."

By 1988, a number of member churches of the WCC had been struck aware by the meaning(s) of the Holocaust. The purely humanitarian concern for decent human relations, which had characterized discussions between Christians and Jews since the founding of the (American) National Conference of Christians and Jews, was giving place to basic theological affirmations of a positive nature that:

- The covenant of God with the Jewish people remains valid;

- Anti-Semitism and all forms of the teaching of contempt for Judaism are to be repudiated;

- The living tradition is a gift of God;

- Coercive proselytism directed toward Jews is incompatible with Christian faith;

- Jews and Christians bear a common responsibility as witness to God's righteousness and peace in the world.[21]

During the 1980s and 1990s, the intellectual encounter of Jews and Christians has worked the most difficult field of all, post-Holocaust: how Christian apologetics may be reformed to affirm the continuing vitality of the Jewish people in their uncancelled covenant with God.

The Content of "We Remember"

From *Nostra Aetate* to "We Remember" is a long march, perhaps especially for a world communion where large sections can easily succumb to the temptation to shrink the Holocaust to the status of "a Jewish affair" or a tragedy pertaining only to the Christians of Europe. To the outsider, the movement of Roman Catholicism seems glacial. Nevertheless it moves (*E pur si muove*), and in this most recent declaration it has moved far beyond Eastern Orthodoxy, and well beyond most of the Protestant and ecumenical entities. Headquarters may be lagging behind the French and German bishops, but it is still well ahead of the Polish bishops!

Let us now direct our attention more precisely to the content of "We Remember":

> Speaking to all Roman Catholics in a worldwide church, confrontation with the Holocaust becomes through "We Remember" a factor in all catechetical instruction, doctrinal and theological considerations.

> Anti-Semitism is roundly condemned, although subsuming it under "racism" removes a large question mark over the church ("guilty of blasphemy") and replaces it with a smaller question mark ("guilty of inhumanity").

> Catholic brothers and sisters are called to renew their awareness of "the Hebrew roots of their faith."

The fact that this horrible crime was committed in countries of long-standing Christian civilization raises the question of a connection between the attitudes of Christians towards the Jews across centuries and the Nazi persecution itself. On balance, the relationship of Christians and Jews over two millennia has been "quite negative."

Hopefully this message of repentance (*teshuva*) will be heard and welcomed by "our Jewish friends" with open hearts.

Certainly the acceptability of the message to Jews will be abetted by a feeling of reciprocal good will for the Vatican recognition of the State of Israel in December of 1993.

To the Christian outsider, the message of "We Remember" includes sections that are jarring to the conscience and to historical perception. Some will be noted here:

• The timing of "We Remember" remains ambiguous, as it was prepared over a decade which also saw the Vatican's highest recognition bestowed upon Maximilian Kolbe and Edith Stein—in both cases an act of minor (?) offence to informed Jews.

• We are told that "the *Shoah* was the work of a thoroughly modern neo-pagan regime." In fact, there were only three members of Hitler's entourage who had severed connection with the church (were registered as legally *ausgetreten*). No one was ever rebuked or disciplined by the churches' authorities. A reference to the "neo-pagan regime" in 1934, or even 1938, would have taken courage—but both the Roman Catholic and the Protestant establishments were then very far from such an act. Sixty years later what does such a term "neo-pagan" really say...about whom? by whom? to whom?

• The injection of an insistent effort to glamorize the record of Pope Pius XII, once the lingering negative perceptions have been stripped away, is literarily disconcerting and factually questionable.[22] That he was informed by a diplomatic rather than a prophetic vision of the Church explains much.[23] His hostility to the Enlightenment and modernity explains more. But it was the lack of nuances in his fear of Bolshevism that brought him to the point where Hitler himself—with his allies in Croatia, Slovenia, Vichy France, Slovakia and elsewhere—was confident that no papal obstacles would be put in the way of his totalitarian and genocidal policies.

• We are told the Church itself was not to blame for violent anti-Semitism and the Holocaust, but rather "some" Christians. We are given the dubious claim that when the Jews were "persecuted" the sum of the Christian record of assistance to the victims was this: "Many did, but others did not." This skirts mendacity: the fact is a few helped, most did not. Yad Vashem keeps count and publicly honors the rescuers that can be identified. If the Vatican archives were opened to scholars a great deal might be cleared up and the true and faithful "Soldiers of the Cross" would stand forth from the haze.

• Again, the inability to contemplate the possibility that the Church as such might err leads to statements that border on Monophysite heresy: i.e., that "the Body of Christ" is only divine and therefore incapable of worldly errors. The "errors and failures" are all attributed to "the sons and daughters of the Church." "At the end of this Millennium the Catholic Church desires to express her deep sorrow for the failures of her sons and daughters in every age." Where did these sons and daughters come from? By whom were they catechized? The painful truth is that they absorbed the religious and cultural anti-Semitism by which they were corrupted from the Church and its teachings across centuries. By failure to distinguish carefully between the theological, cultural, and modern genocidal levels of anti-Semitism,[24]

"We Remember" spreads the guilt in an undifferentiated way that is spiritually and intellectually far more deadly than any "failure" due to ignorance.

Even the French bishops in their generally admirable declaration fall back upon a condemnation of "silence." "...it has to be recognized that the French bishops did not speak out, acquiescing *by their silence* in these flagrant violations of human rights. [...] Too many pastors of the Church *by their silence* offended both against the Church and its mission."[25] Is the old generation passing away so rapidly, the generation that can well remember the Vichy bishops giving the Nazi salute to Petain and Göring?

We are brought to a fundamental difference between Roman Catholicism and Protestantism. Protestants do not confuse the visible church with the spiritual body, and find no more difficulty in criticizing the institution and its leadership than they do any other human institution to which they are tied by covenant and/or affection.

Christendom and the Holocaust

There are two defense mechanisms frequently seen at work when Christian officials attempt to put the Holocaust in place in Church history. One escape is to portray a great Christendom that remained fundamentally intact and survived relatively unscathed, even if with a few scratches on its face. Another escape is to blame the crime of the Holocaust upon a minority of "sons and daughters" who proved unworthy. The institution as such thus remains the pure "Bride of Christ," without flaw or fleck.

The truth is that European "Christendom" is today, as it was in Germany at the time of the Nazis' rise and fall, a hollow shell. Since the 1840s the peoples of the "Christian" nations of Europe have fallen away from their obligations decade by decade. Internal statistical offices tell an entirely different story from the official claims that Italy is "99% Roman Catholic" and Sweden is "96% Lutheran." In the case of Italy the hard figure is less than 10% and in the case of Sweden less than 5%.

Unhappily, the adherents of privileged establishments that are no longer capable of the great acts of faith before the rise of modernity have still shown themselves capable of spreading the violence of war and the venom of anti-Semitism. It is of course no excuse for a "Christendom" that helped produce Nazism, with its pseudo-religious world view and its genocidal politics, that it arose out of an enfeebled Christianity. But the truth must be faced, especially when today we are confronted by a reversion to primitive anti-Semitism in Russian Orthodoxy and a brutal suppression of smaller religious groups (Pentecostals, Jehovah's Witnesses, Scientology—"cults and sects") in parts of Western Europe. The harsh truth is that for some time the "Christian nations" have been *post-Christian*.   .

Six decades ago, with the Jewish people entering into the most traumatic dozen years of its history, Christendom failed both the Jewish neighbors and its own integrity. The very survival of the Jews then hung in the balance. Today we can rejoice that the Lord has delivered His people Israel. Among the many signs of redemption are the State of Israel and the renaissance of energy in the diaspora, especially in the United States of America. Here, so relatively soon after the *Churban*, the largest Jewish community in the world is undergoing a religious, cultural, political, intellectual and economic revival comparable to no other time or place since the destruction of the Second Temple.

At the same time, the legally privileged Christian establishments of Europe and the socially established churches of North America are still struggling to recover in spirit and find a style of life worthy of their calling. They stand, holding "the cup of trembling" (Isa. 51:22-23), their leaders unable in emergency even to count on the loyalty and discipline of their own members.

"We Remember," which is a landmark in the doctrinal development of the Christian understanding of the Holocaust, nevertheless fails in the end to plumb the depths of the present inarticulate post-Auschwitz trauma in Christendom. The message speaks to the world as if it were the Church, and a note of unreality breaks through from time to time.

We are told this is to be a time for the forgiveness of sins and reconciliation with God and neighbor. The latter is a real confrontation; with the former, who is to forgive? The question in Simon Wiesenthal's *The Sunflower*[26] remains unresolved: who wronged whom? who can forgive? who can produce the "fruits worthy of repentance" (Lk. 3:7-8)?

The reason for the feeling of unreality may be that in "We Remember" the discussion of guilt for the Nazi genocide of the Jews, and the descriptions of wrong-doing, are all related in the third person. The result is a presentation of repentance—in the passive voice.

NOTES

1. The intense political maneuvering by both internal and external powers hostile to any "weakening" of traditional Christian hostility toward the Jews, coupled with a determination to influence the Council's pronouncements and follow-up accordingly, is recorded and commented in detail by John M. Oesterreicher in "Declaration on the Relationship of the Church to Non-Christian Religions: Introduction and Commentary," in *Commentary on the Documents of Vatican II*, H. Vorgrimler, ed. (New York: Herder & Herder, 1969), III, 1-136. See also Arthur Gilbert's *The Vatican Council and the Jews* (Cleveland: World Publishing, 1968) and John Oesterreicher's *The New Encounter Between Christians and Jews* (New York: Philosophical Library, 1986).

2. Walter M. Abbott, *The Documents of Vatican II* (New York: Guild Press/America Press, Association Press, 1966), pp. 663-67.

3. The investigation of the Church's high school texts is summarized in the first chapter, and the following chapters discuss the teaching materials' view of Jews, Protestants and racial minorities in John T. Pawlikowski's *Catechetics and Prejudice* (New York: Paulist Press, 1973).

4. Selected from "Toward Renovation of the Relationship of Christians and Jews," a report of synodical actions published in translation in *Journal of Ecumenical Affairs*, Vol. XVII, No. 1 (Winter, 1980), pp. 211-12.

5. *Ibid.*, p. 211.

6. *Dialogues* (a newsletter from the Institute of the World Jewish Congress in Jerusalem), Vol. I, No. 5 (January, 1998), p. 5.

7. The story after the NCCJ passed beyond purely humanitarian and civic emphases has yet to be written. For the beginnings and the early mature years—pre-Auschwitz in thinking—see James E. Pitt, *Adventures in Brotherhood* (New York: Farrar, Straus, 1955).

8. Gideon Hausner, *Justice in Jerusalem* (New York: Harper & Row, 1966).

9. In a few months following the shock of the "Six Day War," three major expressions of Christian-Jewish and Christian post-Auschwitz awareness were founded: 1) the Annual Scholars' Conference on the Holocaust and the Churches; 2) the Christian Study Group on Israel and the Jewish People; 3) the National Christian Leadership Conference for Israel. In all three, the root idea was to advance understanding and affirmation of the survival of the Jewish people. See Franklin H. Littell, "The German Church Struggle and the Holocaust (1970-1990)," in Franklin H. Littell, Alan L. Berger and Hubert G. Locke, eds., *What Have We Learned? Telling the Story and Teaching the Lessons of the Holocaust* (Lewiston/Queenston /Lampeter: Edwin Mellen Press, 1993), pp. 45-57, 54-56.

10. The narrow basis of cooperation was explained by J. Courtney Murray in a small manual circulated under the imprint of the National Catholic Welfare Conference.

11. Bernhard E. Olson, *Faith and Prejudice* (New Haven: Yale University Press, 1963).

12. Gerald S. Strober, *Portrait of the Elder Brother* (New York: AJC/NCCJ, 1972).

13. *Ibid.*, p. 39.

14. Yom Hashoah was first observed sporadically. One of the earliest services was an interreligious event in 1972 in the chapel of Queens College, a Presbyterian school in Charlotte, NC. A volume of *Liturgies on the Holocaust* was edited by Marcia

S. Littell in 1986, and distributed by the Government for use by the chaplains of the Army, Navy and Air Force. A much revised and expanded *Liturgies on the Holocaust*, edited by Marcia S. Littell and Sharon Gutman, was published in 1996 (Trinity Press International, Valley Forge, PA).

15. The 1996 Statement—"Building New Bridges in Hope"—is available in pamphlet form from the General Board of Global Ministries of the United Methodist Church, 7820 Reading Road, Cincinnati, OH 45222-1800.

16. The 1985 Mennonite statement was released by the Home Ministries Department of Eastern Mennonite Board of Missions, Salunga, PA 17538.

17. *Ibid.*, p. 7.

18. Jules Isaac, *Has Anti-Semitism Roots in Christianity?* (New York: National Conference of Christians and Jews, 1961), p. 45. Gentile Christian anti-Semitism is found in official church decrees from the Council of Elvira (309 C.E.), when the rulers of the churches enacted negative legislation against those sectors that made the celibate males most nervous: women, Jews, and "heretics." The Council of Nicaea (325 C.E.), dominated by Constantine and counted the first of the Ecumenical Councils, carried on the developing hostility against the three disfavored elements.

19. *Current Dialogue* (a newsletter of the World Council of Churches' department of "Dialogue with People of Living Faiths"), No. 15 (December, 1988), p. 24.

20. *Ibid.*, p. 23.

21. *Ibid.*, p. 25.

22. For the better part of two decades one of the most able Jesuit fathers, Robert Graham, devoted himself to building a wall between the Pope and responsibility for the Holocaust. See his *Pius XII's Defense of the Jews and Others: 1944-45* (1982). When asked why Adolf Hitler was not checked by the Church, on one occasion Father Graham replied that Hitler was automatically excommunicated when he stood with Hermann Göring at the latter's Protestant wedding in 1931. The Roman Catholic Church is obviously still smarting from the impact of Rolf Hochhuth's *The Deputy*, and it must have seemed to someone that "We Remember" presented a good occasion for a bit of apologetic. The section does not, however, fit the rest of the text.

23. John T. Pawlikowski, "The Vatican and the Holocaust: Putting *We Remember* in Context," *Dimensions*, Vol. XII, No. 2 (1998), p.16.

24. The distinction between religious, cultural, and modern genocidal anti-Semitism is developed *in extenso* in Franklin H. Littell, *The Crucifixion of the Jews* (Macon, GA: Mercer University Press, 1996), paperback of the 1975 Harper & Row linen edition.

25. John T. Pawlikowski, *op. cit.*, p. 13.

26. *The Sunflower*, recently edited in a new edition—on the question of forgiveness—(New York: Schocken Books, 1997), with a symposium edited by Harry James Cargas and Bonnie Fetterman.

5

Reaction of a Jewish Theologian to the Vatican's *We Remember* Document

A. James Rudin

The Vatican's long anticipated document on the Holocaust was published on March 16, 1998. *We Remember: A Reflection on the Shoah* was eagerly awaited by Christians and Jews because the document, first announced in 1987, was to be the Church's formal attempt to directly confront the terrible years of 1933-1945 when the mass murder of Jews was the policy of Nazi Germany. However, *We Remember* raised more questions than it answered, and it created more problems than it solved. It remains a controversial document drawing praise and criticism from both Christians and Jews.

The twelve-page statement is divided into five sections: The Tragedy of the Shoah and the Duty of Remembrance, What We Must Remember, Relations Between Jews and Christians, Nazi Anti-Semitism and the Shoah, and Looking Together to a Common Future. A short but important letter from the Pope to Edward Cardinal Cassidy introduces the document. Cardinal Cassidy, the President of the Pontifical Commission for Religious Relations with the Jews, is the primary author of *We Remember*. The brief papal letter represents John Paul's personal endorsement of the document.

The Pope's letter reveals the Polish-born Pontiff's personal sorrow when he describes "...the sufferings of the Jewish people during the Second World War. The crime which has become known as the Shoah remains an indelible stain on the history of the century that is coming to a close." His words are a refutation of those who deny the reality of the Holocaust as well as those who minimize its horrors. The Pope's letter is one of the positive features of the Vatican document.

John Paul II's words that introduce the 1998 Vatican document are a permanent part of Church teaching. In another context, John Paul II, who was born in 1920 and witnessed first-hand the German occupation of Poland that began in 1939, has declared: "This is the century of the Shoah." I strongly believe that after 1945 the word "Holocaust" must always be spelled with a capital "H" and without a plural ending. Unfortunately, today the term "Holocaust" is being misused when it is employed to describe every terrible event currently taking place. Such continued abuse of the word means that it will soon lose any distinctive meaning. For that reason, I commend the Vatican authors for using the Hebrew term "Shoah," which can only refer to the destruction of six million Jews between 1933 and 1945.

In his letter to Cardinal Cassidy, the Pope calls for "a future in which the unspeakable iniquity of the Shoah will never again be possible." The Pope's words are more powerful than the cautious document that follows. Unlike the Pope's words, *We Remember* is clearly the work of many contributors and it lacks a single compelling voice. The call for remembrance is an integral part of the Pope's teachings and his emphasis on remembering the Shoah has been a hallmark of his pontificate. Since becoming Pope in 1978, John Paul II has consistently stressed the importance of building mutual respect and understanding between Catholics and Jews. His focus on the Shoah was reflected most notably in his 1991 address to Jewish leaders in Budapest. The Pope also reiterated this theme at the 1994 Vatican Concert that commemorated the Shoah. At the conclusion of his remarks at the Concert, the Pope publicly identified with the victims of Nazi German terror, and declared: "Do not forget us!"

The first section of *We Remember* describes the unique bond the Church has with the Jewish people: "...[it] is unlike the one she shares with any other religion. However, it is not only a question of recalling the past. The common future of Jews and Christians demand that we remember, for 'there is no future without memory.' History itself is memoria futuri."

This opening section also calls for "all Christians" to recognize how the "image of the Creator" in human beings "has been offended and disfigured" by the horrors of this century. For Catholics the "unspeakable tragedy [of the Shoah] can never be forgotten." *We Remember* speaks of the necessity to recall the terror of the Holocaust: "Women and men, old and young, children and infants [were murdered].... It is a major fact of the history of this century.... All this was done to them for the sole reason that they were Jews."

Although only three paragraphs in length, the opening section correctly notes that the Shoah "raises many questions," and although "much scholarly study still remains to be done...such an event cannot be fully measured by the ordinary criteria of historical research alone. It calls for a 'moral and religious memory' and, particularly among Christians, a very serious reflection on what gave rise to it [the Shoah]."

The Vatican statement candidly acknowledges that "the Shoah took place in Europe...in countries of long-standing Christian civilization" and it rhetorically asks what influences "the attitudes down the centuries of Christians towards the Jews" had on Nazi German persecutions. Was the Holocaust "made easier by anti-Jewish prejudices embedded in Christian minds and hearts?" Did the centuries of Christian teaching of contempt towards Jews and Judaism make Catholics "less sensitive or even indifferent" to the Shoah?

The document's opening sections pose many of the relevant questions that are addressed later in *We Remember*. The Vatican's call for appropriate remembrance of the Shoah is a strong feature of the entire document. The first two sections of the document reflect the tone and substance of the Pope's letter, and together they accurately spell out its *raison d'être*. However, the remaining sections of *We Remember* are more problematic and troubling than the Pope's letter and the first two sections of the document. The authors of *We Remember* set the proper tone and ask the correct questions at the outset, but then they provide ambivalent, ambiguous, and in some cases unsatisfactory answers. For that reason, *We Remember* is a disappointment to many Catholics and Jews.

The Rev. John T. Pawlikowski, Professor of Social Ethics at the Catholic Theological Union in Chicago, has written that *We Remember* "...is marked by some perspectives which are incomplete and sometimes even misleading." And the Rev. Richard P. McBrien, the Crowley-O'Brien-Walter Professor of Theology at the University of Notre Dame, has declared: "...I believe the weight of the evidence is on the side of the Vatican statement's critics.... By the standards of 1998, the Vatican commission that issued the statement did not go far enough."

The document's various internal contradictions and problems are sharply revealed in the main sections that deal with historic relations between Jews and Christians and with Nazi anti-Semitism and the Shoah. For example, while confessing that the "...history of relations between Jews and Christians is a tormented one," the document also states that the Jewish people "in their devotion to the Law, on occasion violently opposed the preachers of the Gospel and the first Christians."

This unfortunate and unnecessary observation conjures up the old negative canard that has been at heart of much of Christian teaching about Jews and Judaism: the Jews of Jesus' time were wedded to a static vindictive religious "Law" filled with zealotry and restrictions. In contrast, the "preachers of the Gospels," many of whom were of course themselves also Jews, were filled with love and spiritual liberation from the Law's severe yoke. By using the words "violently opposed," the Vatican text transmits the message that a moral equivalency exists between historic, often deadly, Christian persecution and denigration of Jews and Judaism, and the anti-Christian attitudes and behavior of some Jews. It is an equation without an historical basis. Indeed, it was frequently the Church, especially after the First Crusade in 1096, that was the primary source of religious violence. Pagans, Jews, and all other non-Christians were frequently the targets of officially sanctioned "violent" assaults carried out by Christians.

Sadly, this false dichotomy has fostered anti-Jewish attitudes and behavior among many Christians for centuries. In fact, it is precisely this kind of negative teaching that the Roman Catholic Church since the conclusion of the Second Vatican Council in 1965 has been aggressively combating. It is unfortunate that *We Remember*, the Vatican's most important statement on Catholic-Jewish relations since the Council, contains the old, discredited negative reference to the Jewish "Law" and "violent" Jewish opposition to "preachers of the Gospel."

In the same section, the Vatican describes the rise of National Socialism (Nazism) in post World War I Germany. This "extremist form of nationalism" promulgated a "pseudoscientific basis for a distinction between so-called Nordic-Aryan races and supposedly inferior races," especially the Jews. *We Remember* asserts that the "Church in Germany replied by condemning racism." The Vatican document lists some of the Catholic leaders, including Pope Pius XI and Pope Pius XII, who spoke out in the 1930s against Nazi racial ideology. However, the declaration of the German Catholic Bishops issued in January 1995 clearly recognized that such Catholic responses to Nazism in the 1930s were inadequate: "Today the fact is weighing heavily on our mind that individual initiatives [such as those noted in *We Remember*] to help persecuted Jews and that even the pogroms [*Kristallnacht*] of November 1938 were not followed by public and expressed protests; ... [we have as Catholic Bishops] the heavy burden of history…the 'Church which we proclaim as holy and which we all know as a mystery, is also a sinful church and in need of conversion'." This latter statement is from the declaration issued by the German and Austrian bishops' conferences in 1988 on the fiftieth anniversary of the November 1938 pogroms. The forthright statements of the German and Austrian bishops contain a more historically balanced view of the official Catholic responses to Nazi anti-Semitism than does the Vatican document. In addition, there seems to be a tension between the bishops' statements and *We Remember* regarding the behavior of the Church as an church and the behavior of its individual members.

Father McBrien cites the Second Vatican Council's Dogmatic Constitution on the Church (Article 8): "The Church, however, clasping sinners to its bosom, at once holy and always in need of purification, follows constantly the path of penance and renewal." For McBrien "there is no theological or doctrinal impediment to attributing sin to the Church as such in this whole terrible matter of the Shoah and of the Church's complicity in it." McBrien is challenging one of the central themes of *We Remember*: the clear distinction between the Church and the behavior of its members.

In May 1998 Cardinal Cassidy delivered an important address on the Vatican document in Washington, DC, at the Annual Meeting of the American Jewish Committee. In that address the Cardinal said: "This distinction—the Church and the members of the Church—runs throughout the Vatican document and is not readily understood by those who are not members of the Catholic Church. Let me state firstly that when we make this distinction, the term 'members of the church' does not refer to a particular category of church members, but can include according to the circumstances popes, cardinals, bishops, priests, and the laity."

During the same address, Cardinal Cassidy declared: "For Catholics the Church is not just the members that belong to it. It is looked upon as the bride of Christ, the heavenly Jerusalem, holy and sinless." This distinction between the "sinless" Church and "members of the Church" who may act in sinful ways, including genocide, is, of course, an internal Catholic matter. But this distinction is confusing, especially when the German and Austrian Bishops speak of a "sinful Church and in need of conversion" and when the Second Vatican Council speaks of the Church as "always in need of conversion and penance." The section dealing with Nazi anti-Semitism, the Shoah, and the Catholic Church is the heart of *We Remember*, and it is the most problematic. The Vatican document makes a sharp distinction between "anti-Judaism" and "anti-Semitism." The document admits that "Christians have been guilty of anti-Judaism" for centuries, but it carefully removes the Church from the "anti-Semitism" which resulted in the Shoah. Yet the two, anti-Judaism and anti-Semitism, shade into one another and are often indistinguishable.

The document's most surprising, even astonishing statement, reads: "The Shoah was the work of a thoroughly modern neo-pagan regime. Its anti-Semitism had its roots outside of Christianity and, in pursuing its aims, it did not hesitate to oppose the Church and persecute her members also." This statement flies in the face of nearly twenty centuries of anti-Jewish teaching and preaching by many Church leaders. Ironically, ancient paganism was far more tolerant of Jews and Judaism that was the Christian Church.

Throughout history there were countless Christian acts of hatred aimed at Jews, some of which were copied by the Nazis, that included the wearing of the yellow Star of David, the creation of ghettoes, and the teaching that Jews were eternally condemned by God because of their alleged faithlessness in not accepting Jesus as the Messiah. Happily, these ugly teachings were repudiated by the Church beginning in 1965 at the Second Vatican Council, but the desperately needed reforms came twenty years after the end of the Holocaust.

The statement also discounts the vast number of Christian anti-Jewish texts, prohibitions, laws, and acts of discrimination that took one scholar, Heinz Schreckenberg, 2,300 pages to list. Pawlikowski notes that Schreckenberg's work, "The Jew in Christian Art," graphically illustrates how deeply "anti-Semitism permeated Catholic catechesis and preaching and the popular culture it created."

Because Nazi anti-Semitism was racial, it refused to recognize the legitimacy of Jewish conversions to Christianity. Traditional Christian anti-Semitism, in contrast, sought to persecute Jews but always held out the possibility of baptism as a means of "escaping" Judaism. However, even conversion did not always prevent virulent Christian hatred, as the converted Jews in Spain learned during the Inquisition in the fifteenth century.

Pawlikowski sees the clear linkage: "*We Remember* leaves the distinct impression that there is no inherent connection between Nazi ideology and classical anti-Semitism. This is basically inaccurate." The distinction between anti-Judaism and anti-Semitism has also been vigorously criticized by Jewish leaders. Martin S. Kaplan, the American Jewish Committee's Interreligious Affairs Commission Chair, has written: "The Vatican statement thus articulates a vast new problem, seeking to disconnect a thousand years of anti-Jewish behavior and persecution from the Final Solution of the Holocaust, as if a split personality allowed Christians to be anti-Jewish, but once their behavior crossed a certain line in the Holocaust, then they were reflecting their pagan roots."

Following World War II and the Shoah, the French Jewish scholar Jules Isaac coined the term "the teaching of contempt" to describe the systemic pattern of transmitting anti-Semitic teachings to generations of Christians. And the Declaration on the Relationship of the Church to Non-Christian Religions, *Nostra Aetate*, proclaimed on October 28, 1965 at the Second Vatican Council in Rome, emphatically "deplored...all hatred, persecutions and displays of anti-Semitism directed against the Jews at any time and from any source." *We Remember* fails to acknowledge the well-established and well-documented connection between the tragic Christian record of anti-Judaism "down the centuries" and the creation of the cultural and political climate in twentieth century Europe that made the Shoah possible.

In this section of *We Remember*, many important questions are raised, but they are not fully examined. For example: "But it may be asked whether the Nazi persecution of the Jews was not made easier by the anti-Jewish prejudices imbedded in some Christian minds and hearts. Did anti-Jewish sentiment among Christians make them less sensitive, or even indifferent, to the persecutions launched against the Jews by National Socialism...?" Other questions include "Did Christians give every possible assistance to those being persecuted, and in particular to the persecuted Jews?" Unfortunately, *We Remember* provides no clear answers to these and similar questions of faith and behavior. The Vatican document's response to this last question is especially ambiguous: "Many did [give support to persecuted Jews], but others did not." This statement conveys the false impression that the number of Christians who helped Jews during the Shoah was nearly equal to those Christians who were indifferent to the Jewish plight. This is simply not true. The reality is that few Christians actively aided Jews, many participated in the Holocaust persecutions and killings, and the overwhelming majority of European Christians were indifferent to the anti-Jewish actions of the Nazis and their collaborators.

Another troubling aspect of *We Remember* is its ardent defense of the wartime activities of Pope Pius XII. Not surprisingly, this section has drawn sharp criticism. This contentious issue not only involves Jewish critics of the wartime Pope, but also stirs deep passions among Catholics. I regret that *We Remember* includes the defense of Pius XII because it further complicates an already weakened statement. Pius' defense would have been better presented in a separate Vatican document once all the relevant archival documents relating to the World War II Pope had been analyzed by appropriate Catholic and Jewish historians of the period. Because of the crucial importance of Pope Pius XII during the Shoah, it is crucial that competent Catholic and Jewish scholars have full access to the pertinent records. Only in that way can this difficult question be satisfactorily resolved. Those key documents located in Rome and in other parts of Europe which would provide definitive data about Pius XII still remain inaccessible even to qualified scholars. Until and unless the full record is made available by Catholic authorities, all we have is an incomplete and inadequate picture. It is highly problematic when Pius XII's defenders and detractors both make their judgments without full access to the primary source material. Partial information, personal testimonies no matter how sincere, and incomplete data do not make for a strong defense of anyone in history, least of all the spiritual leader of the Roman Catholic Church during World War II. But because the defense of Pius XII is included in *We Remember*, and because that defense relies so heavily upon limited and incomplete records, those holding contrary views of Pius XII vehemently dispute the claims set forth in the Vatican statement.

For example, the Vatican document asserts that "...Jewish communities and leaders expressed their thanks for all that had been done for them, including what Pope Pius XII did personally or through his representatives to save hundreds of thousands of Jewish lives." To support this claim, *We Remember* lists the post World War II testimonies of four prominent Jews, including the late Golda Meir, a Prime Minister of Israel. But there is no attribution nor historical evidence presented for the claim that such a large number of Jews were saved by Pius XII's efforts. Most scholars of the Shoah believe that no one person or institution saved "hundreds of thousands" of people. Without full substantiation of this figure, the Vatican document's claim lacks credibility. In the closing paragraph of this troubling section, the Vatican document lists other horrors of this century including the "massacre of the Armenians,...the Ukraine in the 1930s,...the genocide of the Gypsies,...racist ideas in America, Africa, and the Balkans,...the millions of victims...in the Soviet Union, in China, Cambodia and elsewhere." This clutter of other tragic twentieth century events weakens the intended power of the document. Instead of focusing solely on the Shoah, a menu of atrocities is presented, which weakens the uniqueness of suffering in all the examples cited. Each horrific event needs to be addressed on its own, and should not be added to a genocide stew pertaining to the whole century. This paragraph seems to suggest that the Shoah, an "indelible stain on the history" of this century, cannot be dealt with by and for itself. By specifically listing other fearful events of our time, *We Remember* runs the risk of minimizing them all.

The final sentence of this section is enigmatic and problematic: "Nor can we forget the drama of the Middle East, the elements of which are well known." Which elements? Which drama? Known to whom? Is this a form of compensation and recognition for the Palestinians who are currently engaged in a difficult peace process with Israel, the Jewish state that regained its independence only three years after the Shoah? Since *We Remember* is filled with empathy and solidarity with the Jewish people, did the Vatican authors feel it necessary to "balance" their extraordinary concern for Jews with a veiled acknowledgment of the Palestinians? Is this baffling sentence a backhanded slap at the policies of Israel? Questions abound with no answers. Many people believe this entire paragraph, with its omnibus litany of horrors and its cryptic reference to the Arab-Israeli conflict, was simply tacked onto the original text by Vatican officials who were not among the original drafters of *We Remember*.

The brief closing section of the Vatican document urges Catholics and Jews to work together on issues of mutual concern. It reaffirms Pope John Paul II's 1986 statement made in Rome's Grand Synagogue that Jews are "our elder brothers in faith." Catholics must also work to build a "new relationship " with the Jewish people, one built upon "deep respect and great compassion" as a result of the Shoah.

The section expresses the Church's "deep sorrow for the failures of her sons and daughters in every age. This is an act of repentance (*teshuva*), since...we are linked to the sins as well as the merits of all her [the Church's] children." It also calls for "a firm resolve to build a new future" between Christians and Jews based upon "shared mutual respect." Unfortunately, this otherwise laudable section still retains traces of an inaccurate moral equivalency. In the new century "there will be no more anti-Judaism among Christians or anti-Christian sentiment among Jews, but rather a shared mutual respect...." Surely there is no comparison between Christian anti-Judaism and anti-Semitism, and anti-Christian feelings among Jews. The roles of victimizer and victim are not analogous, and those roles as they have been played out throughout history demand careful clarification and not a facile balancing sentence.

I am disappointed that the document is weaker in tone and substance than the statements on the Shoah issued by the German Bishops in 1995 and the French Bishops in 1997. Those two documents, along with statements made by the Bishops of the United States, Italy, and Poland, are landmark declarations in the long and painful Christian effort to come to terms in a spiritual and theological way with the evil of the Shoah.

Some Vatican officials have publicly explained the apparent discrepancy between the strong national bishops' statements and the weaker *We Remember* document. They note that the Vatican statement is intended for the universal Church, including those areas of the world with little or no Jewish population. They further state that it is precisely the Bishops of Europe, the site of the Shoah, who are best qualified to address the terror of the 1930s and 1940s in all its aspects. In addition, the American Bishops represent the nation that along with its wartime allies played a decisive role in defeating Nazi Germany. However, other Catholic leaders argue that for millions of Catholics, especially in Asia and Africa, *We Remember* may be their only authoritative source of reliable information about Jews, Judaism, and the Shoah. They argue that precisely because *We Remember* is a global document, it should have been as strong and unproblematic as possible.

We Remember is rich with remembrance of past tragic history, it is abundant with calls for repentance, and it is eloquent in its resolve to improve future Catholic-Jewish relations. But the fourth "r," responsibility, is inadequately and incompletely addressed in the document. Indeed, the key word "responsibility" is found only once in the entire document and, not surprisingly, it appears in the Pope's letter of contrition addressed to Cardinal Cassidy: "...The Church... encourages her sons and daughters...to place themselves humbly before the Lord and examine themselves on the responsibility which they too have for the evils of our time." Because of the various limitations and problems of the Vatican document, it is most important that *We Remember* not be the only resource on the Shoah for the world's Catholics. Appropriate new teaching materials, historical research, and liturgical forms are urgently needed to augment and strengthen this Vatican document. Taken by itself, it is an inadequate teaching tool.

Cardinal William Keeler of Baltimore, a former President of the National Conference of Catholic Bishops and a leader in the Catholic-Jewish encounter, and Dr. Eugene Fisher, the NCCB's Director of Catholic-Jewish Relations, recognized this need when, on the day *We Remember* was published, they said: "...we must commit our resources, our historians, sociologists, theologians, and other scholars, as the document mandates, to study together with their Jewish counterparts all the evidence with a view to the healing of memories, a reconciliation of history."

Will *We Remember*, which was so eagerly anticipated, stimulate the intensive Catholic study of "all the evidence" and the contemplation of the Shoah that is urgently required? Or will this well-intentioned but compromised and ambivalent document mark the formal conclusion of the Church's exploration into the Shoah? Only time will tell.

Appendix A

Letter of Pope John Paul II

To my venerable brother, Cardinal Edward Idris Cassidy:

On numerous occasions during my pontificate I have recalled with a sense of deep sorrow the sufferings of the Jewish people during the Second World War. The crime which has become known as the *Shoah* remains an indelible stain on the history of the century that is coming to a close.

As we prepare for the beginning of the third millennium of Christianity, the Church is aware that the joy of a jubilee is above all the joy that is based on the forgiveness of sins and reconciliation with God and neighbor. Therefore she encourages her sons and daughters to purify their hearts through repentance of past errors and infidelities. She calls them to place themselves humbly before the Lord and examine themselves on the responsibility which they too have for the evils of our time.

It is my fervent hope that the document "We Remember: A Reflection on the *Shoah*," which the Commission for Religious Relations with the Jews has prepared under your direction, will indeed help to heal the wounds of past misunderstandings and injustices. May it enable memory to play its necessary part in the process of shaping a future in which the unspeakable iniquity of the *Shoah* will never again be possible. May the Lord of history guide the efforts of Catholics and Jews and all men and women of good will as they work together for a world of true respect for the life and dignity of every human being, for all have been created in the image and likeness of God.

March 12, 1998

We Remember:
A Reflection on the *Shoah*

Holy See's Commission for Religious Relations with the Jews
March 1998

I. TRAGEDY OF THE *SHOAH* AND THE DUTY OF REMEMBRANCE

T he twentieth century is fast coming to a close, and a new millennium of the Christian era is about to dawn. The 2000th anniversary of the birth of Jesus Christ calls all Christians, and indeed invites all men and women, to seek to discern in the passage of history the signs of divine providence at work as well as the ways in which the image of the Creator in man has been offended and disfigured.

This reflection concerns one of the main areas in which Catholics can seriously take to heart the summons which Pope John Paul II has addressed to them in his apostolic letter *Tertio Millennio Adveniente*:

> It is appropriate that as the second millennium of Christianity draws to a close the Church should become more fully conscious of the sinfulness of her children, recalling all those times in history when they departed from the spirit of Christ and his Gospel and, instead of offering to the world the witness of a life inspired by the values of faith, indulged in ways of thinking and acting which were truly forms of counter-witness and scandal.[1]

This century has witnessed an unspeakable tragedy which can never be forgotten: the attempt by the Nazi regime to exterminate the Jewish people, with the consequent killing of millions of Jews. Women and men, old and young, children and infants, for the sole reason of their Jewish origin, were persecuted and deported. Some were killed immediately, while others were degraded, ill-treated, tortured, and utterly robbed of their human dignity, and then murdered. Very few of those who entered the camps survived, and those who did remained scarred for life. This was the *Shoah*. It is a major fact of the history of this century, a fact which still concerns us today.

Before this horrible genocide, which the leaders of nations and Jewish communities themselves found hard to believe at the very moment when it was being mercilessly put into effect, no one can remain indifferent, least of all the Church, by reason of her ver close bonds of spiritual kinship with the Jewish people and her remembrance of the injustices of the past. The Church's relationship to the Jewish people is unlike the one she shares with any other religion.[2] However, it is not only a question of recalling the past. The common future of Jews and Christians demands that we remember, for "there is no future without memory."[3] History itself is *memoria futuri*.

In addressing this reflection to our brothers and sisters of the Catholic Church throughout the world, we ask all Christians to join us in meditating on the catastrophe which befell the Jewish people and on the moral imperative to ensure that never again will selfishness and hatred grow to the point of sowing such suffering and death.[4] Most especially we ask our Jewish friends, "whose terrible fate has become a symbol of the aberrations of which man is capable when he turns against God,"[5] to hear us with open hearts.

II. WHAT WE MUST REMEMBER

While bearing their unique witness to the Holy One of Israel and to the Torah, the Jewish people have suffered much at different times and in many places. But the *Shoah* was certainly the worst suffering of all. The inhumanity with which the Jews were persecuted and massacred during this century is beyond the capacity of words to convey. All this was done to them for the sole reason that they were Jews.

The very magnitude of the crime raises many questions. Historians, sociologists, political philosophers, psychologists, and theologians are all trying to learn more about the reality of the *Shoah* and its causes. Much scholarly study still remains to be done. But such an event cannot be fully measured by the ordinary criteria of historical research alone. It calls for a "moral and religious memory" and, particularly among Christians, a very serious reflection on what gave rise to it.

The fact that the *Shoah* took place in Europe, that is, in countries of long-standing Christian civilization, raises the question of the relation between the Nazi persecution and the attitudes down the centuries of Christians toward the Jews.

III. RELATIONS BETWEEN JEWS AND CHRISTIANS

The history of relations between Jews and Christians is a tormented one. His Holiness Pope John Paul II has recognized this fact in his repeated appeals to Catholics to see where we stand with regard to our relations with the Jewish people.[6] In effect, the balance of these relations over 2,000 years has been quite negative.[7]

At the dawn of Christianity, after the crucifixion of Jesus, there arose disputes between the early Church and the Jewish leaders and people who, in their devotion to the law, on occasion violently opposed the preachers of the Gospel and the first Christians. In the pagan Roman Empire, Jews were legally protected by the privileged granted by the emperor, and the authorities made no distinction between Jewish and Christian communities. Soon, however, Christians incurred the persecution of the state. Later, when the emperors themselves converted to Christianity, they at first continued to guarantee Jewish privileges. But Christian mobs who attacked pagan temples sometimes did the same to synagogues, not without being influenced by certain interpretations of the New Testament regarding the Jewish people as a whole.

"In the Christian world—I do not say on the part of the Church as such—erroneous and unjust interpretations of the New Testament regarding the Jewish people and their alleged culpability have circulated for too long, engendering feelings of hostility toward this people."[8] Such interpretations of the New Testament have been totally and definitively rejected by the Second Vatican Council.[9]

Despite the Christian preaching of love for all, even for one's enemies, the prevailing mentality down the centuries penalized minorities and those who were in any way "different." Sentiments of anti-Judaism in some Christian quarters and the gap which existed between the Church and the Jewish people led to a generalized discrimination, which ended at times in expulsions or attempts at forced conversions. In a large part of the "Christian" world, until the end of the eighteenth century those who were not Christian did not always enjoy a fully guaranteed juridical status. Despite that fact, Jews throughout Christendom held on to their religious traditions and communal customs. They were therefore looked upon with a certain suspicion and mistrust. In times of crisis such as famine, war, pestilence, or social tensions, the Jewish minority was sometimes taken as a scapegoat and became the victim of violence, looting, even massacres.

By the end of the eighteenth century and the beginning of the nineteenth century, Jews generally had achieved an equal standing with other citizens in most states and a certain number of them held influential positions in society. But in that same historical context, notably in the nineteenth century, a false and exacerbated nationalism took hold. In a climate of eventful social change, Jews were often accused of exercising an influence disproportionate to their numbers. Thus there began to spread in varying degrees throughout most of Europe an anti-Judaism that was essentially more sociological and political than religious.

At the same time, theories began to appear which denied the unity of the human race, affirming an original diversity of races. In the twentieth century, National Socialism in Germany used these ideas as a pseudoscientific basis for a distinction between so-called Nordic-Aryan races and supposedly inferior races. Furthermore, an extremist form of nationalism was heightened in Germany by the defeat of 1918 and the demanding conditions imposed by the victors, with the consequence that many saw in National Socialism a solution to their country's problems and cooperated politically with this movement.

The Church in Germany replied by condemning racism. The condemnation first appeared in the preaching of some of the clergy, in the public teaching of the Catholic bishops, and the writings of lay Catholic journalists. Already in February and March 1931, Cardinal Bertram of Breslau, Cardinal Faulhaber and the bishops of Bavaria, the bishops of the province of Cologne, and those of the province of Freiburg published pastoral letters condemning National Socialism, with its idolatry of race and of the state.[10] The well-known Advent sermons of Cardinal Faulhaber in 1933, the very year in which National Socialism came to power, at which not just Catholics but also Protestants and Jews were present clearly expressed rejection of the Nazi antisemitic propaganda.[11] In the wake of the *Kristallnacht*, Bernhard Lichtenberg, provost of Berlin cathedral, offered public prayers for the Jews. He was later to die at Dachau and has been declared blessed.

Pope Pius XI too condemned Nazi racism in a solemn way in his encyclical letter *Mit Brennender Sorge*,[12] which was read in German churches on Passion Sunday 1937, a step which resulted in attacks and sanctions against members of the clergy. Addressing a group of Belgian pilgrims on September 6, 1938, Pius XI asserted: "Antisemitism is unacceptable. Spiritually, we are all Semites."[13] Pius XII, in his very first encyclical, *Summi Pontificatus*[14] of October 20, 1939, warned against theories which denied the unity of the human race and against the deification of the state, all of which he saw as leading to a real "hour of darkness."[15]

IV. NAZI ANTISEMITISM AND THE *SHOAH*

Thus we cannot ignore the difference which exists between *antisemitism*, based on theories contrary to the constant teaching of the Church on the unity of the human race and on the equal dignity of all races and peoples, and the long-standing sentiments of mistrust and hostility that we call *anti-Judaism*, of which, unfortunately, Christians have also been guilty.

The National Socialist ideology went even further, in the sense that it refused to acknowledge any transcendent reality as the source of life and the criterion of moral good. Consequently, a human group, and the state with which it was identified, arrogated to itself an absolute status and determined to remove the very existence of the Jewish people, a people called to witness to the one God and the law of the covenant. At the level of theological reflection we cannot ignore the fact that not a few in the Nazi Party not only showed aversion to the idea of divine providence at work in human affairs, but gave proof of a definite hatred directed at God himself. Logically such an attitude also led to a rejection of Christianity and a desire to see the Church destroyed or at least subjected to the interests of the Nazi state.

It is this extreme ideology which became the basis of the measures taken first to drive the Jews from their homes and then to exterminate them. The *Shoah* was the work of a thoroughly modern neopagan regime. Its antisemitism had its roots outside of Christianity, and in pursuing its aims, it did not hesitate to oppose the Church and persecute her members also.

But it may be asked whether the Nazi persecution of the Jews was not made easier by the anti-Jewish prejudices imbedded in some Christian minds and hearts. Did anti-Jewish sentiment among Christians make them less sensitive or even indifferent to the persecutions launched against the Jews by National Socialism when it reached power?

Any response to this question must take into account that we are dealing with the history of people's attitudes and ways of thinking, subject to multiple influences. Moreover, many people were altogether unaware of the "final solution" that was being put into effect against a whole people; others were afraid for themselves and those near to them; some took advantage of the situation; and still others were moved by envy. A response would need to be given case by case. To do this, however, it is necessary to know what precisely motivated people in a particular situation.

At first the leaders of the Third Reich sought to expel the Jews. Unfortunately, the governments of some western countries of Christian tradition, including some in North and South America, were more than hesitant to open their borders to the persecuted Jews. Although they could not foresee how far the Nazi hierarchs would go in their criminal intentions, the leaders of those nations were aware of the hardships and dangers to which Jews living in the territories of the Third Reich were exposed. The closing of borders to Jewish emigration in those circumstances, whether due to anti-Jewish hostility or suspicion, political cowardice, or shortsightedness, or national selfishness, lays a heavy burden of conscience on the authorities in question.

In the lands where the Nazis undertook mass deportations, the brutality which surrounded these forced movements of helpless people should have led to suspect the worst. Did Christians give every possible assistance to those being persecuted and in particular to the persecuted Jews?

Many did not, but others did. Those who did help to save Jewish lives, as much as was in their power, even to the point of placing their own lives in danger, must not be forgotten. During and after the war, Jewish communities and Jewish leaders expressed their thanks for all that had been done for them, including what Pope Pius XII did personally or through his representatives to save hundreds of thousands of Jewish lives.[16] Many Catholic bishops, priests, religious, and laity have been honored for this reason by the state of Israel.

Nevertheless, as Pope John Paul II has recognized, alongside such courageous men and women, the spiritual resistance and concrete action of other Christians was not that which might have been expected from Christ's followers. We cannot know how many Christians in countries occupied or ruled by the Nazi powers or their allies were horrified at the disappearance of their Jewish neighbors and yet were not strong enough to raise their voices in protest. For Christians, this heavy burden of conscience of their brothers and sisters during the Second World War must be a call to penitence.[17]

We deeply regret the errors and failures of those sons and daughters of the Church. We make our own what is said in the Second Vatican Council's declaration *Nostra Aetate*, which unequivocally affirms: "The Church...mindful of her common patrimony with the Jews, and motivated by the gospel's spiritual love and by no political considerations, deplores the hatred, persecutions, and displays of antisemitism directed against the Jews at any time and from any source."[18]

We recall and abide by what Pope John Paul II, addressing the leaders of the Jewish community in Strasbourg in 1988, stated: "I repeat again with you the strongest condemnation of antisemitism and racism, which are opposed to the principles of Christianity."[19] The Catholic Church therefore repudiates every persecution against a people or human group anywhere, at any time. She absolutely condemns all forms of genocide as well as racist ideologies which give rise to them. Looking back over this century, we are deeply saddened by the violence that has enveloped whole groups of peoples and nations. We recall in particular the massacres of the Armenians, the countless victims in Ukraine in the 1930s, the genocide of the Gypsies, which was also the result of racist ideas, and similar tragedies which have occurred in America, Africa, and the Balkans. Nor do we forget the millions of victims of totalitarian ideology in the Soviet Union, in China, Cambodia, and elsewhere. Nor can we forget the drama of the Middle East, the elements of which are well known. Even as we make this reflection, "many human beings are still their brothers' victims."[20]

V. LOOKING TOGETHER TO A COMMON FUTURE

Looking to the future of relations between Jews and Christians, in the first place we appeal to our Catholic brothers and sisters to renew the awareness of the Hebrew roots of their faith. We ask them to keep in mind that Jesus was a descendant of David; that the Virgin Mary and the apostles belonged to the Jewish people; that the Church draws sustenance from the root of that good olive tree on to which have been grafted the wild olive branches of the gentiles (cf. *Rom* 11:17-24); that the Jews are our dearly beloved brothers, indeed in a certain sense they are "our elder brothers."[21]

At the end of this millennium the Catholic Church desires to express her deep sorrow for the failures of her sons and daughters in every age. This is an act of repentance (*teshuvah*), since as members of the Church we are linked to the sins as well as the merits of all her children. The Church approaches with deep respect and great compassion the experience of extermination, the *Shoah* suffered by the Jewish people during World War II. It is not a matter of mere words, but indeed of binding commitment. "We would risk causing the victims of the most atrocious deaths to die again if we do not have an ardent desire for justice, if we do not commit ourselves to ensure that evil does not prevail over good as it did for millions of the children of the Jewish people. ... Humanity cannot permit all that to happen again."[22]

We pray that our sorrow for the tragedy which the Jewish people has suffered in our century will lead to a new relationship with the Jewish people. We wish to turn awareness of past sins into a firm resolve to build a new future in which there will be no more anti-Judaism among Christians or anti-Christian sentiment among Jews, but rather a shared mutual respect as befits those who adore the one Creator and Lord and have a common father in faith, Abraham.

Finally, we invite all men and women of good will to reflect deeply on the significance of the *Shoah*. The victims in their graves and the survivors through the vivid testimony of what they have suffered have become a loud voice calling the attention of all humanity. To remember this terrible experience is to become fully conscious of the salutary warning it entails: The spoiled seeds of anti-Judaism and antisemitism must never again be allowed to take root in any human heart.

March 16, 1998
Cardinal Edward Idris Cassidy, President
Bishop Pierre Duprey, Vice President
Rev. Remi Hoeckman, OP, Secretary

NOTES

1. John Paul II, apostolic letter, *Tertio Millennio Adveniente. Acta Apostolicae Sedis (AAS)* 87 (1995): 25, no. 33.

2. Cf. John Paul II, speech at the Rome synagogue, April 13, 1986. *AAS* 78 (1986); 1120, no. 4.

3. John Paul II, Angelus prayer, June 11, 1995. *Insegnamenti* 18/1 (1995): 1712.

4. Cf. John Paul II, address to Jewish leaders in Budapest, August 18, 1991. *Insegnamenti* 14/7 (1991): 349, no. 4.

5. John Paul II, encyclical *Centesimus Annus. AAS* 83 (1991): 814-815, no. 17.

6. Cf. John Paul II, address to episcopal conferences; delegates for Catholic-Jewish relations, March 6, 1982. *Insegnamenti* 5/1 (1982): 743-747.

7. Cf. Holy See's Commission for Religious Relations with the Jews, *Notes on the Correct Way to Present the Jews and Judaism in Preaching and Catechesis in the Roman Catholic Church*, June 24, 1985, VI, 1. *Enchiridion Vaticanum* 9, 1656.

8. Cf. John Paul II, speech to symposium on the roots of Anti-Judaism, October 31, 1997. *L'Osservatore Romano* (November 1, 1997): 6, no. 1.

9. Cf. Vatican Council II, *Nostra Aetate*, no. 4.

10. Cf. B. Statiewski, ed., *Akten Deutscher Bischöfe Über die Lage der Kirche, 1933-1945*, Vol. I, 1933-1934 (Mainz, 1968), Appendix.

11. Cf. L. Volk, *Der Bayerische Episkopat und der Nationalsozialismus 1930-1934* (Mainz, 1966), 170-174.

12. The encyclical is dated March 14, 1937. *AAS* 29 (1937): 145-167.

13. *La Documentation Catholique*, 29 (1938): col. 1460.

14. *AAS* 31 (1939): 413-453.

15. *Ibid.*, 449.

16. The wisdom of Pope Pius XII's diplomacy was publicly acknowledged on a number of occasions by representative Jewish organizations and personalities. For example, on September 7, 1945, Dr. Joseph Nathan, who represented the Italian Hebrew Commission, stated: "Above all, we acknowledge the supreme pontiff and the religious men and women who, executing the directives of the Holy Father, recognized the persecuted as their brothers and, with efforts and abnegation, hastened to help us, disregarding the terrible dangers to which they were exposed" (*L'Osservatore Romano* [September 8, 1945]: 2). On September 21 of that same year, Pius XII received in audience Dr. A. Leo Kubowitzki, secretary general of the World Jewish Congress, who came to present "to the Holy Father, in the name of the Union of Israelitic Communities, warmest thanks for the efforts of the Catholic Church on behalf of Jews throughout Europe during the war" (*L'Osservatore Romano* [September 23, 1945]:1). On Thursday, November 29, 1945, the pope met about eighty representatives of Jewish refugees from various concentration camps in Germany, who expressed "their great honor at being able to thank the Holy Father personally for his generosity toward those persecuted during the Nazi-Fascist period" (*L'Osservatore Romano* [November 30, 1945]: 1). In 1958, at the death of Pope Pius XII, Golda Meir sent an eloquent message: "We share in the grief of humanity. When fearful martyrdom came to our people, the voice of the pope was raised for its victims. The life of our times was enriched by a voice speaking out about great moral truths above the tumult of daily conflict. We mourn a great servant of peace."

17. Cf. John Paul II, address to the Federal German Republic's new ambassador to the Holy See, November 8, 1990. *AAS* 83 (1991): 587-588, no. 2.

18. *Nostra Aetate*, no. 4. Translation by Walter M. Abbot, SJ, in *The Documents of Vatican II*.

19. John Paul II, address to Jewish leaders in Strasbourg, October 9, 1988. *Insegnamenti* 11/3 (1988): 1134, no. 8.

20. John Paul II, address to the diplomatic corps, January 15, 1994. *AAS* 86 (1994): 816, no. 9.

21. John Paul II, Rome synagogue speech, no. 4.

22. John Paul II, address at a commemoration of the *Shoah*, April 7, 1994. *Insegnamenti* 171 (1994): 897 and 893, no. 3.

Appendix B

Ecumenical Council Vatican II

"Declaration on the Relationship of the Church to Non-Christian Religions," *Nostra Aetate* (no. 4) (October 28, 1965).

As this sacred Synod searches into the mystery of the Church, it recalls the spiritual bond linking the people of the New Covenant with Abraham's stock.

For the Church of Christ acknowledges that, according to the mystery of God's saving design, the beginnings of her faith and her election are already found among the patriarchs, Moses, and the prophets. She professes that all who believe in Christ, Abraham's sons according to faith (cf. *Ga* 3:7), are included in the same patriarch's call, and likewise that the salvation of the church was mystically foreshadowed by the chosen people's exodus from the land of bondage.

The Church, therefore, cannot forget that she received the revelation of the Old Testament through the people with whom God in His inexpressible mercy deigned to establish the Ancient Covenant. Nor can she forget that she draws sustenance from the root of that good olive tree onto which have been grafted the wild olive branches of the Gentiles (cf. *Rm* 11:17-24). Indeed, the Church believes that by His cross Christ, our Peace, reconciled Jew and Gentile, making them both one in Himself (cf. *Ep* 2:14-16).

Also, the Church ever keeps in mind the words of the Apostle about his kinsmen, "who have the adoption as sons, and the glory and the covenant and the legislation and the worship and the promise; who have the fathers, and from whom is Christ according to the flesh" (*Rm* 9:4-5), the son of the Virgin Mary. The Church recalls too that from the Jewish people sprang the apostles, her foundation stones and pillars, as well as most of the early disciples who proclaimed Christ to the world.

As holy Scripture testifies, Jerusalem did not recognize the time of her visitation (cf. *Lk* 19:44), nor did the Jews in large number accept the gospel; indeed, not a few opposed the spreading of it (cf. *Rm* 11:28). Nevertheless, according to the Apostle, the Jews still remain most dear to God because of their fathers, for He does not repent of the gifts He makes nor of the calls He issues (cf. *Rm* 11:28-29). In company with the prophets and the same Apostle, the Church awaits that day, known to God alone, on which all peoples will address the Lord in a single voice and "serve Him with one accord" (*Soph* 3:9; cf. *Is* 66:23; *Ps* 65:4; *Rm* 11:11-32).

Since the spiritual patrimony common to Christians and Jews is thus so great, this sacred Synod wishes to foster and recommend that mutual understanding and respect which is the fruit above all of biblical and theological studies, and of brotherly dialogues.

True, authorities of the Jews and those who followed their lead pressed for the death of Christ (cf. *Jn* 19:6); still, what happened in His passion cannot be blamed upon all the Jews then living, without distinction, nor upon the Jews of today. Although the Church is the new people of God, the Jews should not be presented as repudiated or cursed by God, as if such views followed from the holy Scriptures. All should take pains, then, lest in catechetical instruction and in the preaching of God's Word they teach anything out of harmony with the truth of the gospel and the spirit of Christ.

The Church repudiates all persecutions against any man. Moreover, mindful of her common patrimony with the Jews, and motivated by the gospel's spiritual love and by no political considerations, she deplores the hatred, persecutions, and displays of anti-Semitism directed against the Jews at any time and from any source.

Besides, as the Church has always held and continues to hold, Christ in His boundless love freely underwent His passion and death because of the sins of all men, so that all might attain salvation. It is, therefore, the duty of the Church's preaching to proclaim the cross of Christ as the sign of God's all-embracing love and as the fountain from which every grace flows.

Appendix C

Commission for Religious Relations with the Jews

"Guidelines and Suggestions for Implementing the Conciliar Declaration *Nostra Aetate* (no. 4)" (December 1, 1974).

Introductory note

The document is published over the signature of Cardinal Willebrands, in his capacity as President of the new Commission for the Catholic Church's religions relations with the Jews, instituted by Paul IV on 22 October 1974. It comes out a short time after the ninth anniversary of the promulgation of *Nostra Aetate*, the Second Vatican Council's Declaration on the Church's relations with non-Christian religions.

The "Guidelines and Suggestions," which refer to no. 4 of the Declaration, are notable for their almost exclusively practical nature and for their sobriety.

This deliberately practical nature of the text is justified by the fact that it concerns a pragmatic document.

It does not propose a Christian theology of Judaism. Such a theology certainly has an interest for specialist research and reflection, but it still needs considerable study. The new Commission for Religions Relations with the Jews should be able to play a part in the gradual fruition of this endeavor.

The *first part* of the Document recalls the principal teachings of the Council on the condemnation of anti-semitism and of all discrimination, and the obligation of reciprocal understanding and of renewed mutual esteem. It also hopes for a better knowledge on the part of Christians of the essence of the religious tradition of Judaism and of the manner in which Jews identify themselves.

The text then proposes a series of concrete suggestions.

113

The section dedicated to *dialogue* calls for fraternal dialogue and the establishment of deep doctrinal research. Prayer in common is also proposed as a means of encounter.

With regard to the *liturgy*, mention is made of the links between the Christian liturgy and the Jewish liturgy and of the caution which is needed in dealing with commentaries on biblical texts, and with liturgical explanations and translations.

The part concerning *teaching* and *education* allows the relations between the two touched upon and stress is laid on the note of expectation which characterizes both the Jewish and Christian religion. Specialists are invited to conduct serious research and the establishment of chairs of Hebrew studies is encouraged where it is possible, as well as collaboration with Jewish scholars.

The final section deals with the possibilities of *common social action* in the context of a search for social justice and for peace.

The *conclusion* touches on, among other things, the ecumenical aspect of the problem of relations with Judaism, the initiatives of local churches in this area, and the essential lines of the mission of the new Commission instituted by the Holy See.

The great sobriety of the text is noted also in the concrete suggestions which it puts forward. But it would certainly be wrong to interpret such sobriety as being indicative of a limiting programme of activities. The document does propose limited suggestions for some key sectors, but it is a document meant for the universal Church, and as such it cannot take account of all the individual situations. The suggestions put forward are intended to give ideas to those who were asking themselves how to start on a local level that dialogue which the text invites them to begin and to develop. These suggestions are mentioned because of their value as examples. They are made because it seems that they could find ample application and that their proposal at the same time constitutes an apt programme for aiding local churches to organize their own activities, in order to harmonize with the general movement of the universal Church in dialogue with Judaism.

The Document can be considered from a certain point of view as the Commission's first step for the realization of religious relations with Judaism. It will devolve on the new Commission to prepare and put forward, when necessary, the further developments which may seem necessary in order that the initiative of the Second Vatican Council in this important area may continue to bear fruit on a local and worldwide level, for the benefit of peace of heart and harmony of spirit of all who work under the protection of the one Almighty God.

The Document, which gives the invitation to an effort of mutual understanding and collaboration, coincides with the opening of the Holy Year, which is consecrated to the theme of reconciliation. It is impossible not to perceive in such a coincidence an invitation to study and to apply in concrete terms throughout the whole world the suggestions which the Document proposes. Likewise one cannot fail to hope that our Jewish brothers too may find in it useful indications for their participation in a commitment which is common.

* * *

Preamble

The Declaration *Nostra Aetate*, issued by the Second Vatican Council on 28 October 1965, "on the relationship of the Church to non-Christian religions" (no. 4), marks an important milestone in the history of Jewish-Christian relations.

Moreover, the step taken by the Council finds its historical setting in circumstances deeply affected by the memory of the persecution and massacre of Jews which took place in Europe just before and during the Second World War.

Although Christianity sprang from Judaism, taking from it certain essential elements of its faith and divine cult, the gap dividing them was deepened more and more, to such an extent that Christian and Jew hardly knew each other.

After two thousand years, too often marked by mutual ignorance and frequent confrontation, the Declaration *Nostra Aetate* provides an opportunity to open or to continue a dialogue with a view to better mutual understanding. Over the past nine years, many steps in this direction have been taken in various countries. As a result, it is easier to distinguish the conditions under which a new relationship between Jews and Christians may be worked out and developed. This seems the right moment to propose, following the guidelines of the Council, some concrete suggestions born of experience, hoping that they will help to bring into actual existence in the life of the Church the intentions expressed in the conciliar document.

While referring the reader back to this document, we may simply restate here that the spiritual bonds and historical links binding the Church to Judaism condemn (as opposed to the very spirit of Christianity) all forms of anti-semitism and discrimination, which in any case the dignity of the human person alone would suffice to condemn. Further still, these links and relationships render obligatory a better mutual understanding and renewed mutual esteem. On the practical level in particular, Christians must therefore strive to acquire a better knowledge of the basic components of the religious tradition of Judaism; they must strive to learn by what essential traits the Jews define themselves in the light of their own religious experience.

With due respect for such matters of principle, we simply propose some first practical applications in different essential areas of the Church's life, with a view to launching or developing sound relations between Catholics and their Jewish brothers.

I. *Dialogue*

To tell the truth, such relations as there have been between Jew and Christian have scarcely ever risen above the level of monologue. From now on, real dialogue must be established.

Dialogue presupposes that each side wishes to know the other, and wishes to increase and deepen its knowledge of the other. It constitutes a particularly suitable means of favouring a better mutual knowledge and, especially in the case of dialogue between Jews and Christians, of probing the riches of one's own tradition. Dialogue demands respect for the other as he is; above all, respect for his faith and his religious convictions.

In the virtue of her divine mission, and her very nature, the Church must preach Jesus Christ to the world (*Ad Gentes*, 2). Lest the witness of Catholics to Jesus Christ should give offence to Jews, they must take care to live and spread their Christian faith while maintaining the strictest respect for religious liberty in line with the teaching of the Second Vatican Council (Declaration *Dignitatis Humanae*). They will likewise strive to understand the difficulties which arise for the Jewish soul—rightly imbued with an extremely high, pure notion of the divine transcendence—when faced with the mystery of the incarnate Word.

While it is true that a widespread air of suspicion, inspired by an unfortunate past, is still dominant in this particular area, Christians, for their part, will be able to see to what extent the responsibility is theirs and deduce practical considerations for the future.

In addition to friendly talks, competent people will be encouraged to meet and to study together the many problems deriving from the fundamental convictions of Judaism and of Christianity. In order not to hurt (even involuntarily) those taking part, it will be vital to guarantee, not only tact, but a great openness of spirit and diffidence with respect to one's own prejudices.

In whatever circumstances as shall prove possible and mutually acceptable, one might encourage a common meeting in the presence of God, in prayer and silent meditation, a highly efficacious way of finding that humility, that openness of heart and mind, necessary prerequisites for a deep knowledge of oneself and of others. In particular, that will be done in connection with great causes such as the struggle for peace and justice.

II. *Liturgy*

The existing links between the Christian liturgy and the Jewish liturgy will be borne in mind. The idea of a living community in the service of God, and in the service of men for the love of God, such as it is realized in the liturgy, is just as characteristic of the Jewish liturgy as it is of the Christian one. To improve Jewish-Christian relations, it is important to take cognizance of those common elements of the liturgical life (formula, feasts, rites, etc.) in which the Bible holds an essential place.

An effort will be made to acquire a better understanding of whatever in the Old Testament retains its own perpetual value (cf. *Dei Verbum*, 14-15), since that has not been cancelled by the later interpretation of the New Testament. Rather, the New Testament brings out the full meaning of the Old, while both Old and New illumine and explain each other (cf. *ibid.*, 16). This is all the more important since liturgical reform is now bringing the text of the Old Testament ever more frequently to the attention of Christians.

When commenting on biblical texts, emphasis will be laid on the continuity of our faith with that of the earlier Covenant, in the perspective of the promises, without minimizing those elements of Christianity which are original. We believe that those promises were fulfilled with the first coming of Christ. But it is none the less true that we still await their perfect fulfillment in his glorious return at the end of time.

With respect to liturgical readings, care will be taken to see that homilies based on them will not distort their meaning, especially when it is a question of passages which seem to show the Jewish people as such in an unfavourable light. Efforts will be made so to instruct the Christian people that they will understand the true interpretation of all the texts and their meaning for the contemporary believer.

Commissions entrusted with the task of liturgical translation will pay particular attention to the way in which they express those phrases and passages which Christians, if not well informed, might misunderstand because of prejudice. Obviously, one cannot alter the text of the Bible. The point is that, with a version destined for liturgical use, there should be an overriding preoccupation to bring out explicitly the meaning of a text,[1] while taking scriptural studies into account.

The preceding remarks also apply to introductions to biblical readings, to the Prayer of the Faithful, and to commentaries printed in missals used by the laity.

III. *Teaching and Education*

Although there is still a great deal of work to be done, a better understanding of Judaism itself and its relationship to Christianity has been achieved in recent years thanks to the teaching of the Church, the study and research of scholars, as also to the beginning of the dialogue.

In this respect, the following facts deserve to be recalled:

— It is the same God, "inspirer and author of the books of both Testaments" (*Dei Verbum*, 16), who speaks both in the old and new Covenants.

— Judaism in the time of Christ and the Apostles was a complex reality, embracing many different trends, many spiritual, religious, social and cultural values.

— The Old Testament and the Jewish tradition founded upon it must not be set against the New Testament in such a way that the former seems to constitute a religion of only justice, fear and legalism, with no appeal to the love of God and neighbour (cf. *Dt* 6:5; *Lv* 19:18; *Mt* 22:34-40).

— Jesus was born of the Jewish people, as were his Apostles and a large number of his first disciples. When he revealed himself as the Messiah and Son of God (cf. *Mt* 16:16), the bearer of the new Gospel message, he did so in fulfillment and perfection of the earlier Revelation. And, although his teaching had a profoundly new character, Christ, nevertheless, in many instances, took his stand on the teaching of the Old Testament. The New Testament is profoundly marked by its relation to the Old. As the Second Vatican Council declared: "God, the inspirer and author of the books of both Testaments, wisely arranged that the New Testament be hidden in the Old and the Old be made manifest in the New" (*Dei Verbum*, 16). Jesus also used teaching methods similar to those employed by the rabbis of his time.

With regard to the trial and death of Jesus, the Council recalled that "what happened in his passion cannot be blamed upon all the Jews then living, without distinction, nor upon the Jews of today" (*Nostra Aetate*, 4).

— The history of Judaism did not end with the destruction of Jerusalem, but rather went on to develop a religious tradition. And, although we believe that the importance and meaning of that tradition were deeply affected by the coming of Christ, it is still nonetheless rich in religious values.

— With the prophets and the apostle Paul, "the Church awaits the day, known to God alone, on which all peoples will address the Lord in a single voice and 'serve him with one accord' (*Soph* 3:9)" (*Nostra Aetate*, 4).

Information concerning these questions is important at all levels of Christian instruction and education. Among sources of information, special attention should be paid to the following:

— catechism and religious textbooks;
— history books;
— the mass-media (press, radio, cinema, television).

The effective use of these means presupposes the thorough formation of instructors and educators in training schools, seminaries and universities.

Research into the problems bearing on Judaism and Jewish-Christian relations will be encouraged among specialists, particularly in the fields of exegesis, theology, history and sociology. Higher institutions of Catholic research, in association if possible with other similar Christian institutions and experts, are invited to contribute to the solution of such problems. Wherever possible, chairs of Jewish studies will be created, and collaboration with Jewish scholars encouraged.

IV. *Joint Social Action*

Jewish and Christian tradition, founded on the Word of God, is aware of the value of the human person, the image of God. Love of the same God must show itself in effective action for the good of mankind. In the spirit of the prophets, Jews and Christians will work willingly together, seeking social justice and peace at every level—local, national and international.

At the same time, such collaboration can do much to foster mutual understanding and esteem.

Conclusion

The Second Vatican Council has pointed out the path to follow in promoting deep fellowship between Jews and Christians. But there is still a long road ahead.

The problem of Jewish-Christian relations concerns the Church as such, since it is when "pondering her own mystery" that she encounters the mystery of Israel. Therefore, even in areas where no Jewish communities exist, this remains an important problem. There is also an ecumenical aspect to the question: the very return of

Christians to the sources and origins of their faith, grafted on to the earlier Covenant, helps the search for unity in Christ, the cornerstone.

In this field, the bishops will know what best to do on the pastoral level, within the general disciplinary framework of the Church and in line with the common teaching of her magisterium. For example, they will create some suitable commissions or secretariats on a national or regional level, or appoint some competent person to promote the implementation of the conciliar directives and the suggestions made above.

On 22 October 1974, the Holy Father instituted for the universal Church this Commission for Religious Relations with the Jews, joined to the Secretariat for Promoting Christian Unity. This special Commission, created to encourage and foster religious relations between Jews and Catholics—and to do so eventually in collaboration with other Christians—will be, within the limits of its competence, at the service of all interested organizations, providing information for them, and helping them to pursue their task in conformity with the instructions of the Holy See.

The Commission wishes to develop this collaboration in order to implement, correctly and effectively, the express intentions of the Council.

Given at Rome, 1 December 1974.

✠ JOHANNES Card. WILLEBRANDS
President of the Commission

Pierre-Marie de Contenson, OP
Secretary of the Commission

NOTES

1. Thus the formula "the Jews," in St. John, sometimes according to the context means "the leaders of the Jews," or "the adversaries of Jesus," terms which express better the thought of the evangelist and avoid appearing to arraign the Jewish people as such. Another example is the use of the words "pharisee" and "pharisaism" which have taken on a largely pejorative meaning.

Appendix D

Commission for Religious Relations with the Jews

"Notes on the correct way to present the Jews and Judaism in preaching and catechesis in the Roman Catholic Church" (June 24, 1985)

Preliminary Considerations

On March 6th, 1982, Pope John Paul II told delegates of episcopal conferences and other experts, meeting in Rome to study relations between the Church and Judaism:

"...you yourselves were concerned, during your sessions, with Catholic teaching and catechesis regarding Jews and Judaism.... We should aim, in this field, that Catholic teaching at its different levels, in catechesis to children and young people, presents Jews and Judaism, not only in an honest and objective manner, free from prejudices and without any offences, but also with full awareness of the heritage common" to Jews and Christians.

In this passage, so charged with meaning, the Holy Father plainly drew inspiration from the Council Declaration *Nostra Aetate*, 4, which says:

"All should take pains, then, lest in catechetical instruction and in the preaching of God's Word they teach anything out of harmony with the truth of the Gospel and the spirit of Christ"; as also from these words: "Since the spiritual patrimony common to Christians and Jews is thus so great, this sacred Synod wishes to foster and recommend mutual understanding and respect...."

In the same way, the *Guidelines and Suggestions for Implementing the Conciliar Declaration Nostra Aetate (no. 4)* ends its chapter III, "Teaching and Education," which lists a number of practical things to be done, with this recommendation:

"Information concerning these questions is important at all levels of Christian instruction and education. Among sources of information, special attention should be paid to the following:

— catechisms and religious textbooks;
— history books;
— the mass media (press, radio, cinema, television).

The effective use of these means presupposes the thorough formation of instructors and educators in training schools, seminaries and universities" (*AAS* 77 [1975] 73).

The paragraphs which follow are intended to serve this purpose.

I
RELIGIOUS TEACHING AND JUDAISM

1. In *Nostra Aetate*, 4, the Council speaks of the "spiritual bonds linking" Jews and Christians and of the "great spiritual patrimony" common to both and it further asserts that "the Church of Christ acknowledges that, according to the mystery of God's saving design, the beginning of her faith and her election are already found among the patriarchs, Moses and the prophets."

2. Because of the unique relations that exist between Christianity and Judaism—"linked together at the very level of their identity" (John Paul II, 6th March, 1982)—relations "founded on the design of the God of the Covenant" (*ibid.*), the Jews and Judaism should not occupy an occasional and marginal place in catechesis: their presence there is essential and should be organically integrated.

3. This concern for Judaism in Catholic teaching has not merely a historical or archeological foundation. As the Holy Father said in the speech already quoted, after he had again mentioned the "common patrimony" of the Church and Judaism as "considerable": "To assess it carefully in itself and with due awareness of the faith and religious life of the Jewish people *as they are professed and practiced still today*, can greatly help us to understand better certain aspects of the life of the Church" (underlining added). It is a question then of *pastoral* concern for a still living reality closely related to the Church. The Holy Father has stated this permanent reality of the Jewish people in a remarkable theological formula, in his allocution to the Jewish community of West Germany at Mainz, on November 17th, 1980:

"...the people of God of the Old Covenant, which has never been revoked...."

4. Here we should recall the passage in which the *Guidelines and Suggestions*, I, tried to define the fundamental condition of dialogue: "respect for the other as he is," knowledge of the "basic components of the religious tradition of Judaism" and again learning "by what essential traits the Jews define themselves in the light of their own religious experience" (*Introd.*).

5. The singular character and the difficulty of Christian teaching about Jews and Judaism lies in this, that it needs to balance a number of pairs of ideas which express the relation between the two economies of the Old and New Testament:

Promise and Fulfillment
Continuity and Newness
Singularity and Universality
Uniqueness and Exemplary Nature.

This means that the theologian and the catechist who deals with the subject needs to show in his practice of teaching that:

— promise and fulfillment throw light on each other;
— newness lies in a metamorphosis of what was there before;
— the singularity of the people of the Old Testament is not exclusive and is open, in the divine vision, to a universal extension;
— the uniqueness of the Jewish people is meant to have the force of an example.

6. Finally, "work that is of poor quality and lacking in precision would be extremely detrimental to Judaeo-Christian dialogue (John Paul II, speech of March 6th, 1982). But it would be above detrimental—since we are talking of teaching and education—to Christian identity (*ibid.*).

7. "In virtue of her divine mission, the Church" which is to be "the all-embracing means of salvation" in which alone "the fullness of the means of salvation can be obtained" (*Unitatis Redintegratio*, 3), "must of her nature proclaim Jesus Christ to the world" (cf. *Guide-*

lines and Suggestions, I). Indeed we believe that it is through Him that we go to the Father (cf. *Jn* 14:6) "and this is eternal life, that they know Thee the only true God and Jesus Christ whom Thou hast sent" (*Jn* 17:3).

Jesus affirms (*ibid.* 10:16) that "there shall be one flock and one shepherd." Church and Judaism cannot then be seen as two parallel ways of salvation and the Church must witness to Christ as the Redeemer for all, "while maintaining the strictest respect for religious liberty in line with the teaching of the Second Vatican Council (Declaration *Dignitatis Humanae*" (*Guidelines and Suggestions*, I).

8. The urgency and importance of precise, objective and rigorously accurate teaching on Judaism for our faithful follows too from the danger of anti-Semitism which is always ready to reappear under different guises. The question is not merely to uproot but much rather to arouse in them, through educational work, an exact knowledge of the wholly unique "bond" (*Nostra Aetate*, 4) which joins us as a Church to the Jews and to Judaism. In this way, they would learn to appreciate and love the latter, who have been chosen by God to prepare the coming of Christ and have preserved everything that was progressively revealed and given in the course of that preparation, notwithstanding their difficulty in recognising in Him their Messiah.

II
RELATIONS BETWEEN THE OLD[1] AND NEW TESTAMENT

1. Our aim should be to show the unity of Biblical Revelation (O.T. and N.T.) and of the divine plan, before speaking of each historical event, so as to stress that particular events have meaning when seen in history as a whole—from creation to fulfillment. This history concerns the whole human race and especially believers. Thus the definitive meaning of the election of Israel does not become clear except in the light of the complete fulfillment (*Rm* 9-11) and election in Jesus Christ is still better understood with reference to the announcement and the promise (cf. *Heb* 4:1-11).

2. We are dealing with singular happenings which concern a singular nation but are destined, in the sight of God who reveals His purpose, to take on universal and exemplary significance.

The aim is moreover to present the events of the Old Testament not as concerning only the Jews but also touching us personally. Abraham is truly the father of our faith (cf. *Rm* 4:11-12; Roman Canon: *patriarchae nostri Abrahae*). And it is said (*1 Co* 10:1): "*Our* fathers were all under the cloud, and all passed through the sea." The patriarchs, prophets and other personalities of the Old Testament have been venerated and always will be venerated as saints in the liturgical tradition of the Oriental Church as also of the Latin Church.

3. From the unity of the divine plan derives the problem of the relation between the Old and New Testaments. The Church already from apostolic times (cf. *1 Co* 10:11; *Heb* 10:1) and then constantly in tradition resolved this problem by means of typology, which emphasises the primordial value that the Old Testament must have in the Christian view. Typology, however, makes many people uneasy and is perhaps the sign of a problem unresolved.

4. Hence, in using typology, the teaching and practice which we have received from the Liturgy and from the Fathers of the Church, we should be careful to avoid any transition from the Old to the New Testament which might seem merely a rupture. The Church, in the spontaneity of the Spirit which animates her, has vigorously condemned the attitude of Marcion[2] and always opposed his dualism.

5. It should be emphasised that typological interpretation consists in reading the Old Testament as preparation and, in certain aspects, outline and foreshadowing of the New (cf., e.g., *Heb* 5:5-10, etc.). Christ is henceforth the key and point of reference to the Scriptures: "the rock *was* Christ" (*1 Co* 10:4).

6. It is true then, and should be stressed, that the Church and Christians read the Old Testament in the light of the event of the dead and risen Christ and that on these grounds there is a Christian reading of the Old Testament which does not necessarily coincide with the Jewish reading. Thus Christian identity and Jewish identity should be carefully distinguished in their respective reading of the Bible. But

this detracts nothing from the value of the Old Testament in the Church and does nothing to hinder Christians from profiting discerningly from the traditions of Jewish reading.

7. Typological reading only manifests the unfathomable riches of the Old Testament, its inexhaustible content and the mystery of which it is full, and should not lead us to forget that it retains its own value as Revelation that the New Testament often does no more than resume (cf. *Mk* 12:29-31). Moreover, the New Testament itself demands to be read in the light of the Old. Primitive Christian catechesis constantly had recourse to this (cf., e.g., *1 Co* 5:6-8; 10:1-11).

8. Typology further signifies reaching towards the accomplishment of the divine plan, when "God will be all in all" (*1 Cor* 15:28). This holds true also for the Church which, realised already in Christ, yet awaits its definitive perfecting as the Body of Christ. The fact that the Body of Christ is still tending towards its full stature (cf. *Ep* 4:12-19) takes nothing from the value of being a Christian. So also the calling of the patriarchs and the Exodus from Egypt do not lose their importance and value in God's design from being at the same time intermediate stages (cf., e.g., *Nostra Aetate*, 4).

9. The Exodus, for example, represents an experience of salvation and liberation that is not complete in itself, but has in it, over and above its own meaning, the capacity to be developed further. Salvation and liberation are already accomplished in Christ and gradually realised by the sacraments in the Church. This makes way for the fulfillment of God's design, which awaits its final consummation with the return of Jesus as Messiah, for which we pray each day. The Kingdom, for the coming of which we also pray each day, will be finally established. With salvation and liberation the elect and the whole of Creation will be transformed in Christ (*Rm* 8:19-23).

10. Furthermore, in underlining the eschatological dimension of Christianity we shall reach a greater awareness that the people of the Old and the New Testament are tending towards a like end in the future: the coming or returning of the Messiah—even if they start from two different points of view. It is more clearly understood that the person of the Messiah is not only a point of division for the people

of God but also a point of convergence (cf. *Sussidi per l'ecumenismo* of the diocese of Rome, n. 140). Thus it can be said that Jews and Christians meet in a comparable hope, founded on the same promise made to Abraham (cf. *Gn* 12:1-3; *Heb* 6:13-18).

11. Attentive to the same God who has spoken, hanging on the same word, we have to witness to one same memory and one common hope in Him who is the master of history. We must also accept our responsibility to prepare the world for the coming of the Messiah by working together for social justice, respect for the rights of persons and nations and for social and international reconciliation. To this we are driven, Jews and Christians, by the command to love our neighbour, by a common hope for the Kingdom of God and by the great heritage of the Prophets. Transmitted soon enough by catechesis, such a conception would teach young Christians in a practical way to cooperate with Jews, going beyond simple dialogue (cf. *Guidelines*, IV).

III
JEWISH ROOTS OF CHRISTIANITY

12. Jesus was and always remained a Jew, his ministry was deliberately limited "to the lost sheep of the house of Israel" (*Mt* 15:24). Jesus is fully a man of his time, and of his environment—the Jewish Palestinian one of the first century, the anxieties and hopes of which he shared. This cannot but underline both the reality of the Incarnation and the very meaning of the history of salvation, as it has been revealed in the Bible (cf. *Rm* 1:3-4; *Ga* 4:4-5).

13. Jesus' relations with biblical law and its more or less traditional interpretations are undoubtedly complex and he showed great liberty towards it (cf. the "antitheses" of the Sermon on the Mount: *Mt* 5:21-48, bearing in mind the exegetical difficulties; his attitude to rigorous observance of the Sabbath: *Mk* 3:1-6, etc.).

But there is no doubt that he wished to submit himself to the law (cf. *Ga* 4:4), that he was circumcised and presented in the Temple like any Jew of his time (cf. *Lk* 2:21. 22-24), that he was trained in the law's observance. He extolled respect for it (cf. *Mt* 5:17-20) and invited obedience to it (cf. *Mt* 8:4). The rhythm of his life was marked by observance of pilgrimages on great feasts, even from his infancy (cf. *Lk* 2:41-50; *Jn* 2:13; 7-10, etc.). The importance of the cycle of the Jewish feasts has been frequently underlined in the Gospel of John (cf. 2:13; 5:1; 7:2.10.37; 10:22; 12:1; 13:1; 18:28; 19:42, etc.).

14. It should be noted also that Jesus often taught in the Synagogues (cf. *Mt* 4:23; 9:35; *Lk* 4:15-18; *Jn* 18:20, etc.) and in the Temple (cf. *Jn* 18:20, etc.), which he frequented as did the disciples even after the Resurrection (cf., e.g., *Ac* 2;46; 3:1; 21:26, etc.). He wished to put in the context of synagogue worship the proclamation of his Messiahship (cf. *Lk* 4:16-21). But above all he wished to achieve the supreme act of the gift of himself in the setting of the domestic liturgy of the Passover, or at least of the paschal festivity (cf. *Mk* 14:1.12 and parallels; *Jn* 18:28). This also allows of a better understanding of the "memorial" character of the Eucharist.

15. Thus the Son of God is incarnate in a people and a human family (cf. *Ga* 4:4; *Rm* 9:5). This takes away nothing, quite the contrary, from the fact that he was born for all men (Jewish shepherd and pagan wise men are found at his crib: *Lk* 2:8-20; *Mt* 2:1-12) and died for all men (at the foot of the cross there are Jews, among them Mary and John: *Jn* 19:25-27, and pagans like the centurion: *Mk* 15:39 and parallels). Thus he made two peoples one in his flesh (cf. *Ep* 2:14-17). This explains why with the *Ecclesia ex gentibus* we have, in Palestine and elsewhere, an *Ecclesia ex circumcisione*, of which *Eusebius* for example speaks (*H.E.*, IV, 5).

16. His relations with the Pharisees were not always or wholly polemical. Of this there are many proofs:

— It is Pharisees who warn Jesus of the risks he is running (*Lk* 13:31);
— Some Pharisees are praised—e.g., "the scribe" of *Mk* 12:34;
— Jesus eats with Pharisees (*Lk* 7:36; 14:1).

17. Jesus shares, with the majority of Palestinian Jews of that time, some pharisaic doctrines: the resurrection of the body; forms of piety, like alms-giving, prayer, fasting (cf. *Mt* 6:1-18) and the liturgical practice of addressing God as Father; the priority of the

commandment to love God and our neighbour (cf. *Mk* 12:28-34). This is also with Paul (cf. *Ac* 23:8), who always considered his membership of the Pharisees as a title of honour (cf. *ibid.*, 23:6; 26:5; *Ph* 3:5).

18. Paul also, like Jesus himself, used methods of reading and interpreting Scripture and of teaching his disciples which were common to the Pharisees of their time. This applies to the use of parables in Jesus' ministry, as also to the method of Jesus and Paul of supporting a conclusion with a quotation from Scripture.

19. It is noteworthy too that the Pharisees are not mentioned in accounts of the Passion. Gamaliel (*Ac* 5:34-39) defends the apostles in a meeting of the Sanhedrin. An exclusively negative picture of the Pharisees is likely to be inaccurate and unjust (cf. *Guidelines*, Note 1; cf. *AAS*, p. 76). If in the Gospel and elsewhere in the New Testament there are all sorts of unfavourable references to the Pharisees, they should be seen against the background of a complex and diversified movement. Criticisms of various types of Pharisees are moreover not lacking in rabbinical sources (cf. the *Babylonian Talmud*, the *Sotah* treatise 22b, etc.). "Phariseeism" in the pejorative sense can be rife in any religion. It may also be stressed that, if Jesus shows himself severe towards the Pharisees, it is because he is closer to them than to other contemporary Jewish groups (cf. *supra*, no. 17).

20. All this should help us to understand better what St. Paul says (*Rm* 11:16 ff.) about the "root" and the "branches." The Church and Christianity, for all their novelty, find their origin in the Jewish milieu of the first century of our era, and more deeply still in the "design of God" (*Nostra Aetate*, 4), realised in the Patriarchs, Moses and the Prophets (*ibid.*), down to its consummation in Christ Jesus.

IV
THE JEWS IN THE NEW TESTAMENT

21. The *Guidelines* already say (note 1) that "the formula 'the Jews' sometimes, according to the context, means 'the leaders of the Jews' or 'the adversaries of Jesus,' terms which express better the thought of the evangelist and avoid appearing to arraign the Jewish people as such."

An objective presentation of the role of the Jewish people in the New Testament should take account of these various facts:

A) The Gospels are the outcome of long and complicated editorial work. The dogmatic constitution *Dei Verbum*, following the Pontifical Biblical Commission's Instruction *Sancta Mater Ecclesia*, distinguished three stages: "The sacred authors wrote the four Gospels, selecting some things from the many which had been handed on by word of mouth or in writing, reducing some of them to a synthesis, explicating some things in view of the situation of their Churches, and preserving the form of proclamation, but always in such fashion that they told us the honest truth about Jesus" (no. 19).

Hence it cannot be ruled out that some references hostile or less than favourable to the Jews have their historical context in conflicts between the nascent Church and the Jewish community. Certain controversies reflect Christian-Jewish relations long after the time of Jesus.

To establish this is of capital importance if we wish to bring out the meaning of certain Gospel texts for the Christians of today.

All this should be taken into account when preparing catechesis and homilies for the last weeks of Lent and Holy Week (cf. already *Guidelines* II, and now also *Sussidi per l'ecumenismo nella diocesi di Roma*, 1982, 144b).

B) It is clear on the other hand that there were conflicts between Jesus and certain categories of Jews of his time, among them Pharisees, from the beginning of his ministry (cf. *Mk* 2:1-11.24; 3:6, etc.)

C) There is moreover the sad fact that the majority of the Jewish people and its authorities did not believe in Jesus—a fact not merely of history but of theological bearing, of which St. Paul tries hard to plumb the meaning (*Rm* chap. 9-11).

D) This fact, accentuated as the Christian mission developed, especially among the pagans, led inevitably to a rupture between Judaism and the young Church, now irreducibly separated and divergent in faith, and this stage of affairs is reflected in the texts of the New Testament and particularly in the Gospels. There is no question of playing down or glossing over this rupture; that could only prejudice the identity of either side. Nevertheless it certainly does not cancel the spiritual "bond" of which the Council speaks (*Nostra Aetate*, 4) and which we propose to dwell on here.

E) Reflecting on this in the light of Scripture, notably of the chapters cited from the epistle to the Romans, Christians should never forget that the faith is a free gift of God (cf. *Rm* 9:12) and that we should never judge the consciences of others. St. Paul's exhortation "do not boast" in your attitude to "the root" (*Rm* 11:18) has its full point here.

F) There is no putting the Jews who knew Jesus and did not believe in him, or those who opposed the preaching of the apostles, on the same plane with Jews who came after or those of today. If the responsibility of the former remains a mystery hidden with God (cf. *Rm* 11:25), the latter are in an entirely different situation. Vatican II in the declaration on *Religious Liberty* teaches that "all men are to be immune from coercion...in such wise that in matters religious no one is to be forced to act in manner contrary to his own beliefs. Nor...restrained from acting in accordance with his own beliefs" (no. 2). This is one of the bases—proclaimed by the Council—on which Judaeo-Christian dialogue rests.

22. The delicate question of responsibility for the death of Christ must be looked at from the standpoint of the conciliar declaration *Nostra Aetate*, 4 and of *Guidelines and Suggestions* (§ III): "What happened in (Christ's) passion cannot be blamed upon all the Jews then living without distinction nor upon the Jews of today," especially since "authorities of the Jews and those who followed their lead pressed for the death of Christ." Again, further on: "Christ in his boundless love freely underwent his passion and death because of the sins of all men, so that all might attain salvation" (*Nostra Aetate*, 4). The *Catechism* of the Council of Trent teaches that Christian sinners are more to blame for the death of Christ than those few Jews who brought it about—they indeed "knew not what they did" (cf. *Lk* 23:34) and we know it only too well (Pars I, caput V, Quaest. XI). In the same way and for the same reason, "the Jews should not be presented as repudiated or cursed by God, as if such views followed from the

holy Scriptures" (*Nostra Aetate*, 4), even though it is true that "the Church is the new people of God" (*ibid.*).

V
THE LITURGY

23. Jews and Christians find in the Bible the very substance of their liturgy: for the proclamation of God's word, response to it, prayer of praise and intercession for the living and the dead, recourse to the divine mercy. The Liturgy of the word in its own structure originates in Judaism. The prayer of Hours and other liturgical texts and formularies have their parallels in Judaism as do the very formulas of our most venerable prayers, among them the Our Father. The eucharistic prayers also draw inspiration from models in the Jewish tradition. As John Paul II said (Allocution of March 6th, 1982): "...the faith and religious life of the Jewish people as they are professed and practised still today, can greatly help us to understand better certain aspects of the life of the Church. Such is the case of liturgy...."

24. This is particularly evident in the great feasts of the liturgical year, like the Passover. Christians and Jews celebrate the Passover: the Jews, the historic Passover looking towards the future; the Christians, the Passover accomplished in the death and resurrection of Christ, although still in expectation of the final consummation (cf. *supra* no. 9). It is still the "memorial" which comes to us from the Jewish tradition, with a specific content different in each case. On either side, however, there is a like dynamism: for Christians it gives meaning to the eucharistic celebration (cf. the antiphon *O sacrum convivium*), a paschal celebration and as such a making present of the past, but experienced in the expectation of what is to come.

VI
JUDAISM AND CHRISTIANITY IN HISTORY

25. The history of Israel did not end in 70 A.D. (cf. *Guidelines*, II). It continued, especially in a numerous Diaspora which allowed Israel to carry to the whole world a witness—often heroic—of its

fidelity to the one God and to "exalt Him in the presence of all the living" (*Tobit* 13:4), while preserving the memory of the land of their forefathers at the heart of their hope (Passover *Seder*).

Christians are invited to understand this religious attachment which finds its roots in Biblical tradition, without however making their own any particular religious interpretation of this relationship (cf. *Declaration* of the US Conference of Catholic Bishops, November 20, 1975).

The existence of the State of Israel and its political options should be envisaged not in a perspective which is in itself religious, but in their reference to the common principles of international law.

The permanence of Israel (while so many ancient peoples have disappeared without trace) is a historic fact and a sign to be interpreted within God's design. We must in any case rid ourselves of the traditional idea of a people *punished*, preserved as a *living argument* for Christian apologetic. It remains a chosen people, "the pure olive on which were grafted the branches of the wild olive which are the gentiles" (John Paul II, 6th March 1982, alluding to *Rm* 11:17-24). We must remember how much the balance of relations between Jews and Christians over two thousand years has been negative. We must remind ourselves of how the permanence of Israel is accompanied by a continuous spiritual fecundity, in the rabbinical period, in the Middle Ages and in modern times, taking its start from a patrimony which we long shared, so much so that "the faith and religious life of the Jewish people as they are professed and practised still today, can greatly help us to understand better certain aspects of the life of the Church" (John Paul II, March 6th, 1982). Catechesis should on the other hand help in understanding the meaning for the Jews of the extermination during the years 1939-1945, and its consequences.

26. Education and catechesis should concern themselves with the problem of racism, still active in different forms of anti-Semitism. The Council presented it thus: "Moreover, (the Church) mindful of her common patrimony with the Jews and motivated by the Gospel's spiritual love and by no political considerations, deplores the hatred, persecutions and displays of anti-Semitism directed against the Jews at any time and from any source" (*Nostra Aetate*, 4). The *Guidelines*

comment: "The spiritual bonds and historical links binding the Church to Judaism condemn (as opposed to the very spirit of Christianity) all forms of anti-Semitism and discrimination, which in any case the dignity of the human person alone would suffice to condemn" (*Guidelines*, Preamble).

CONCLUSION

27. Religious teaching, catechesis and preaching should be a preparation not only for objectivity, justice, tolerance but also for understanding and dialogue. Our two traditions are so related that they cannot ignore each other. Mutual knowledge must be encouraged at every level. There is evident in particular a painful ignorance of the history and traditions of Judaism, of which only negative aspects and often caricature seem to form part of the stock ideas of many Christians.

That is what these notes aim to remedy. This would mean that the Council text and *"Guidelines and Suggestions"* would be more easily and faithfully put into practice.

JOHANNES Cardinal WILLEBRANDS
President

PIERRE DUPREY
Vice-President

JORGE MEJÍA
Secretary

NOTES

1. We continue to use the expression *Old Testament* because it is traditional (cf. already *2 Co* 3:14) but also because "Old" does not mean "out of date" or "outworn." In any case, it is the *permanent* value of the O.T. as a source of Christian Revelation that is emphasised here (cf. *Dei Verbum*, 3).

2. A man of gnostic tendency who in the second century rejected the Old Testament and part of the New as the world of an evil god, a demiurge. The Church reacted strongly against the heresy (cf. Irenaeus).

Contributors

Randolph L. Braham is Distinguished Professor Emeritus of Political Science at The City College and the Doctoral Program at the Graduate School and University Center of the City University of New York, where he also serves as Director of the Rosenthal Institute for Holocaust Studies. He is the author or editor of many monographs, including *The Politics of Genocide. The Holocaust in Hungary* (1981; 2d ed. 1994).

Franklin H. Littell is Distinguished Professor of Holocaust Studies at the Richard Stockton College of New Jersey. An Emeritus Professor of Religion at Temple University, Dr. Littell is the author of several monographs, including *The Crucifixion of the Jews* (1986) and *The German Church Struggle and the Holocaust* (with Hubert G. Locke; 1974).

Hyam Maccoby is a fellow of the Leo Baeck College of London, where he teaches Talmud, Aramaic, and Apocrypha. He is the author of many highly acclaimed monographs, including *Revolution in Judaea* (1980), *The Sacred Executioner* (1983), and *A Pariah People: The Anthropology of Antisemitism* (1996). His *Judas Iscariot and the Myth of Jewish Evil* (1992) was awarded the prestigious Wingate Prize.

John F. Morley is Professor of Religious Studies at Seton Hall University, South Orange, NJ, where he also serves as Minister to the Priest Community, and as a member of the Advisory Council of the Institute of Judaeo-Christian Studies. Reverend Morley is the author of *Vatican Diplomacy and the Jews During the Holocaust, 1939-1943* (1980), and of many scholarly articles. His forthcoming book is titled *Vatican Diplomacy and the Jews of Hungary During the Holocaust.*

A. James Rudin is National Director of Interreligious Affairs of the American Jewish Committee. He is the author of *Israel for Christians: Understanding Modern Israel* (1983), and co-editor of *Evangelicals and Jews in Conversation* (1978) and *A Time to Speak: The Evangelical-Jewish Encounter* (1987). Rabbi Rudin also published many articles in highly respected periodicals.

HOLOCAUST STUDIES SERIES

Randolph L. Braham, Editor
The Institute for Holocaust Studies
The Graduate School and University Center
The City University of New York

Previously published books in the Series:
Perspectives on the Holocaust, 1982
Contemporary Views on the Holocaust, 1983
Genocide and Retribution, 1983
The Hungarian Jewish Catastrophe: A Selected and Annotated Bibliography, 1984
Jewish Leadership During the Nazi Era: Patterns of Behavior in the Free World, 1985
The Holocaust in Hungary — Forty Years Later, 1985
The Origins of the Holocaust: Christian Anti-Semitism, 1985
The Halutz Resistance in Hungary, 1942–1944, 1986
The Tragedy of Hungarian Jewry: Essays, Documents, Depositions, 1986
The Treatment of the Holocaust in Textbooks, 1987
The Psychological Perspectives of the Holocaust and of Its Aftermath, 1988
Reflections of the Holocaust in Art and Literature, 1990
Studies on the Holocaust in Hungary, 1990
Anti-Semitism and the Treatment of the Holocaust in Postcommunist Eastern Europe, 1994
The Tragedy of Romanian Jewry, 1994
The Wartime System of Labor Service in Hungary, 1995
The Holocaust in Hungary: Fifty Years Later, 1997
The Destruction of Romanian and Ukrainian Jews during the Antonescu Era, 1997
The Romanian Nationalists and the Holocaust: The Political Exploitation of Unfounded Rescue Accounts, 1998
Studies on the Holocaust: Selected Writings, Vol. 1, 2000

The Holocaust Studies Series is published in cooperation with the Institute for Holocaust Studies. These books are outgrowths of lectures, conferences, and research projects sponsored by the Institute. It is the purpose of the Series to subject the events and circumstances of the Holocaust to scrutiny by a variety of academics who bring different scholarly disciplines to the study.

The first three books in the Series were published by
Kluwer–Nijhoff Publishing of Boston